Pyramind

TRAINING SERIES

Welcome to the Music Business

S0-BYG-661

Alfred Music Publishing Co., Inc.
Los Angeles

Alfred Music Publishing Co., Inc., Los Angeles

ISBN-10: 0-7390-7195-5 Book & DVD
ISBN-13: 978-0-7390-7195-3 Book & DVD

Interior by Stephen Ramirez.

Edited by Sarah Jones and George Petersen.

Cover photograph by Trevor Traynor.

Produced in Association with Lawson Music Media, Inc., Nashville, TN
www.lawsonmusicmedia.com

Contents

Section 1
The Entrepreneurial Nature of the Music Business
by Gregory J. Gordon

Section 2
Success Strategies
by Tess Taylor

Acknowledgements

Everyone at Pyramind knows that we're a part of a larger musical community. As part of that whole, we've learned that no art is created alone. It's the people around us that make the art special. These books are the result of the work of all the good people in the Pyramind community. From the authors, to the graphic designers and audio collectors, to all of the support staff that keeps the place humming day in and day out, these works represent the collected efforts of our entire team.

There are some teammates who deserve special mention for their extra efforts and dedication in providing this high-quality product for you, our special customer! It's been a pleasure to work with all of them at Pyramind and I am extremely proud of every contributor. I've listed them here to give them a written pat on the back and heartfelt thanks for everything they've done—both for this project and for Pyramind every day.

Thank you!

—Matt Donner
mix and mastering engineer, author, teacher, producer,
CAO Pyramind, project manager, guitarist, bassist, pianist

At Pyramind

Paul Terry:	author, guest lecturer
Tess Taylor:	author, guest lecturer, president NARIP
Steffen Franz:	author, teacher, producer, president IDC
Gregory J. Gordon:	author, producer, engineer, CEO and founder of Pyramind & Epiphyte Records, voice actor and singer
Steve Heithecker:	author, chief engineer, Pro Tools expert, art director, teacher, producer, keyboardist

At Large

George Petersen:	editor, coach and all-around awesome dude
Mike Lawson:	executive producer and another all-around awesome dude
Stephen Ramirez:	art director, book design

Preface

Over my 17-year career, I witnessed radical changes in all the many aspects of the sound industry. The artistry has changed, the business has changed and the technology has certainly changed—the only thing that hasn't changed is sound itself!

These days, technology has never been so powerful and affordable. Newcomers to music and audio production have the lowest cost of entry ever with more power per dollar coming every year! We're continually bombarded with cool new hardware products that become "must-have" items for studios and producers, and much of that hardware stays valuable for life. In fact, some of the most-prized studio microphones and outboard processors are more than 50 years old! On the other hand, manufacturers of digital software tools debut amazing new versions every eight to twelve months, so keeping up is both an exciting and challenging process! While each version may only last a year or so, the tools become more powerful and easier to use with each release. Fortunately, many newcomers to audio production are already technically savvy, and can readily understand the software and achieve solid results quickly.

This is an exciting time to become involved with music/audio production due to the access to such power, yet there's never been a harder time to get started. The tools are affordable; building a professional music and audio production studio used to cost millions of dollars for the gear alone—never mind the cost of building the space! These days, a professional rig can be assembled for roughly $25,000 and semi-professional and hobbyist studios (we call them "project" studios) can come together for less than $5,000! But just because you can build it, doesn't mean they will come. You've got the same tools as 25 other producers on your block, but what makes *you* so special? Why should someone pay *you*?

The world of music and audio production is like a diamond—it may be dazzling and brilliant, with dozens of facets to stare at, but it's really only one stone. If you stare at one facet only, you'll miss the others. By simply twisting the diamond a bit, a whole new set of colors is presented, making it seem like a whole new stone—but it's not. Once you've seen the whole stone, facet-by-facet, you truly understand what you're seeing.

Many people in our industry simply stare at one facet thinking they have the diamond nailed. Most often, it's the technology facet. Users get lost in the features and functions of their gear and forget about the listener. But simply having the tools does not make you successful—you need to understand the whole process behind productions that succeeded before making it a career. In other words, you've got to keep twisting the diamond to see *all* the facets before truly knowing it.

We Made These Books for Producers

To describe the producer's role, you have to describe the production process. It usually starts at the artist with the song. Good producers work the song with the artist to script the flow of the song, the instruments that will play and the performance nuances so a certain sonic goal can be achieved. From the rehearsal space, the producer takes the artist and project into the studio to work with an audio engineer. Afterwards, the producer takes the final product and moves it to the market. This can be in conjunction with a label or manager, but isn't always that way. Long and short, the producer's job is to take this song idea, produce a recording and then market it.

This is *not* what an audio engineer does. Audio engineers have a fairly clear job description. They're responsible for the capture, manipulation and delivery of audio. That job starts and ends in the studio while the producer's job started long before the studio and ends long after it. Producers have the widest responsibility set and they usually take a good portion of the song and production ownership for their efforts and risk. Theirs is also the most complex, as it involves aspects of songwriting, engineering, marketing, sales and a whole lot of personality management—to name a few!

We at Pyramind have been doing this a long time and already made the mistakes most producers make as they begin their careers. What makes us unique? We offer a world-class training program, partnered with the industry's leading manufacturers and we produce music and audio all day, every day. We practice everything we preach for our clients because it works. Now, we are presenting our knowledge to you here in these books.

Why Create a Book Series?

☛ Getting information is easy but getting the right information is hard. The Internet has no shortage of "how to" examples. However, for every 20 free videos, you'll be lucky if one will give you a clue about what to do in your situation. There's no way to get personalized coaching from videos—especially free ones! That's why we hire coaches and mentors, go to school, etc. Books can be hard to learn from because they "tell you," rather than teach you. Knowing what something is doesn't tell you how to use it—these books are meant to give you the tools to using the information. After all, the results are all that matter so knowing the tech talk is useless until you can actually use it!

☛ We want to be your "on-call" coaches. We've done this long enough to know that there are no right answers for every situation and the only method that really works for you is yours. We always say there are four ways to do things— the right way, the wrong way, the Pyramind way and your way. Good coaches help you develop your own sense of workflow based on your creativity so that you can make the right call every time. Until the time when you're ready to craft your own workflow, you can just use ours to get through—they work every time.

☛ Writing these books helps us give back to our community in ways we weren't lucky enough to have when we were learning this stuff! From our self-earned knowledge, we've become excellent at teaching—a very different skill from simply knowing or even doing. A good teacher creates a framework for you to operate under until you're ready to operate on your own. These books offer just that framework.

☛ Selfishly, we want better producers out there. Music and audio production is a glorious art form and we all deserve great art. We also believe that there's an artist in each of us. Having the tools and simply stapling loops together doesn't make great art—it makes collage art. We want to hear what you think—not what the presets think.

☞ We want to buck the "starving musician" category. We make great music that everyone should enjoy. Music makes our lives richer and artists should be paid for their works. This is not a podium rant on the state of file sharing; rather it's the overall comment that says "music is valuable" and creating it can be a viable career. In fact, some people become wildly rich in our business! It's not just a pipedream—there are real opportunities out there if you're willing to bust your hump to get it.

How to Use These Books

When completed, this series comprise nine books in three levels—beginning, intermediate and advanced—with books on creative, technical and business in each group. We believe that the blend of all three of these disciplines is the key to success in our industry. Having wild creativity won't move your career forward if you can't execute your ideas. And if you can execute your wild ideas, if you misunderstand the music-purchasing marketplace, you won't earn any money. And without money, you can't buy more gear.

The best way to use these books is to have them all, one level at a time. You can't separate the creative and technical aspects of a project—these must work together to achieve a goal. You can't separate the creative and business sides, either—making something great and selling it to no one does nothing for your career. Having a great idea for a piece of music and having the market to sell it to won't do you any good if it doesn't sound good when you release it. We know–we've made all of these mistakes ourselves and we see others making the same mistakes every day.

Having each of the three disciplines (creativity, technology and business) in an easy-to-digest form with references to each other is the best way to provide the teaching and coaching we want to give. We love to teach, we're extremely focused on giving real-world, practical, highly effective training to our students and we wanted to offer the same approach here.

These books are written in plain language—we're not trying to dazzle you with facts, figures or overly technical information in an effort to show you how smart we are. In fact, how smart *we* are doesn't even matter! The only thing that matters is *your* results—making *you* smarter about how and "why" you work.

The language is used to help you get into the information easily and put it to use. Knowing the difference between dB SPL and dBfs is great—as long as it has some application that can make your productions sound better. Otherwise, it's just jargon—words that get tossed around at conferences to make people look like they know what they're doing.

Keep in mind that some information will be duplicated across the three. This helps reinforce the commonality of the subjects and the information itself.

One of our training techniques is cross-referenced learning, which means that hearing the same thing three times from three teachers in three different classes should tell you that something is true—and it's something your really need to know. By covering the same subject across each of the books, your understanding of the material (the "why") is much greater than just reading it once.

By that same reasoning, some of the same material is occasionally covered more than once within each title. In this case, you're getting the same information—or something similar—from two or more sources. Each book has several authors covering the subject, each presenting facets of the diamond in their way.

We hope that you enjoy these books and more importantly—that you find them useful. If this first series covers information you already know, then congratulations—you're ready for the next series! It's likely that even if you already know this information, there's bound to be a few nuggets of wisdom that you didn't have at the start. We always have students who already have a lot of experience, yet we find that their body of homegrown knowledge is made up of little "bubbles" of knowledge with thin connections between them. These books are the perfect for these folks to help erase the boundaries of the little bubbles and make one big bubble out of them. So even if you know many of the pieces, these books should help you wrap all of this knowledge up into a single body of knowledge you can use every day.

And we hope that your productions shine as brightly as a diamond!

—Matt Donner

Introduction: Some Insights into Gregory J. Gordon

Many people have the delusion that the music business runs on great music—it doesn't. It runs on people. If great music was the sole benchmark of success, then all of your favorite artists would be household names and their records would be dipped in gold. Clearly, this is not the case. So being good is not enough—you've got to be smart and you've got to know people.

I've been partnered with Greg Gordon at Pyramind since January 1, 2000. What a way to start a new millennia! When I first joined the company in 1996, I was a freelance engineer looking for a studio to call home. Being new to the San Francisco area, creating my professional network was slow going—people here wanted to know what I had done in SF, not NYC (my home town). It's a beautiful Catch-22 of business—how could I have SF experience if I'd only been in town for a few months?

Greg had a different response—he said "Okay, kid—get in there and show me what you got." I did. We've worked together ever since.

The point here is twofold—one, everyone deserves a first shot at success. Being that you're likely looking for your first shot, don't be surprised if people start giving you the old Catch-22 along with a "we'll keep your résumé on file." Persistence is the key here. Greg wasn't the first person I looked up—he was closer to the twentieth. That was because at the time, Pyramind was a small studio and I was looking to the biggest studios first.

The second point here is when that shot comes, be ready. The Chinese call it "being lucky." We do, too. The definition of luck here is "the marriage of opportunity and preparedness"—i.e., being in the right place at the right time *and* being ready.

One of the things that continually impresses me about Greg is how he manages his relationships. Greg is a well-connected guy in this business—as a board member of the San Francisco Chapter of the Recording Academy and someone who was elected by his peers to represent them as a Trustee to The National Academy Of Recording Arts & Sciences (the Grammy organization), he is among the "who's who" of the music business, particularly in San Francisco. Greg always has a positive outlook on business, he's always honorable in his dealings with people and he avoids over-promising—something that runs rampant in the business.

His writing is simple and straightforward, although his career was not! This book begins with his overview of the business in general, careers to be had in this industry—there are lots—and Greg presents a positive, hopeful outlook on the music business in general.

I second his recommendation to read the book *The Diamond Cutter* by Gesha Michael Roach. It was tremendously valuable for both of us in how we approach business and our community as a whole. It takes a very holistic and clean approach to business and its principles have served us well at Pyramind. Mostly, it shows that you can be nice and still win—something the music business could use a lot more of.

—Matt Donner

CHAPTER 1

Time to Go To Work

DVD: Studio-Side Chat
Chapter 1: The New Face of
the Music Business
Intro: 00–43
A shrinkage of the business,
history of slow-moving
industry: 44–3:53

At Pyramind, we often say that there are three functions of the music business that lead to success more than others—luck, opportunity and an open mind—although these terms may not mean exactly what you think they mean! Let me explain.

I have often heard it said that it is easier to win the lottery than it is to find financial success in the music industry. Many say that it requires a tremendous amount of luck to succeed in this business and there are others who will tell you there is no such thing as luck.

I will respond that luck is 50 percent being in the right place at the right time and the other 50 percent is simply being ready for the opportunity when it presents itself—the marriage of opportunity and preparedness. Being "ready" is never the result of any one action but a culmination of much preparation and determination. Being in the right place at the right time almost always has to do with whom you choose to surround yourself with. Realizing your potential in any endeavor is challenging and at its core is being able to understand the secret of how things really work—and how to work with people as passionate as yourself (whether or not you agree with them!).

For the vast majority, a new wave of independence has created opportunities for artists to have much more control over their careers than within the major label system. As new technologies converge, we expect a demising of old ways of doing business from which new opportunities arise. The individuals or companies adapting to these rapid changes are those who are seeing the hidden potentials in new technology and how society responds to this technology. This is creating a rebirth or restructuring of our industry, focused on independence and self-sufficiency. We see an evolution in our industry as a result of all of these forces and have branded our company accordingly—"Pyramind Studios—Evolving Sound".

I will be proving this point throughout this writing.

The music business is an industry where college degrees and formal training are not necessarily required. It attracts a diverse cast of "do it yourself" (DIY) characters each vying to make their mark. In order to be successful with the DIY approach, one is faced with the task of mastering a dizzying amount of skills and talents required to create, produce, distribute and market both recorded and live music performances.

COACH'S CORNER: Wisdom from *The Diamond Cutter*

"The secret of how things really work, the secret to achieving true and lasting success in our everyday lives and our business endeavors, is something deep, and not easily seen without effort. But it is certainly worth the effort." —from *The Diamond Cutter*, by Michael Roach, page 20.

This line comes from the translation of an ancient text (*The Diamond Cutter*, updated into modern settings by Mr. Roach from the ancient text) believed to be the oldest dated book in the world that was printed—not written out by hand. A certain British museum holds a copy that dates from 868 A.D., or about 600 years before the Gutenberg Bible was produced. At its core, the significance of this text is a deep understanding of the hidden potential in all things—not just that of your talent, but of all the opportunities we are presented with in our lives.

"Look through a window pane made of a D-color diamond ("D" is the best or most colorless stone...) and it would look totally clear. If there were a wall of diamonds several feet wide between you and another person, and if no light were reflecting from its surface, you couldn't see the diamond at all... Diamonds represent, in the ancient Tibetan way, a hidden potential in all things: This is usually referred to as "emptiness." A businessperson who is fully aware of this potential thereby understands the very key for attaining success, both in financial and personal terms." —from *The Diamond Cutter*, by Michael Roach, page 14.

This "hidden potential" is alive and well in the music industry. There are many who lament the demise of the "industry" and who claim that the "golden age of music" is behind us and that music has lost its value in a deluge of Internet piracy and digital cloning of files. This may be true, but only for the relatively few who've navigated their way to success within the major record label system.

With so many hats to wear, it's easy to see how one can become distracted trying to focus on one specific task. I have met many a would-be recording artist who set out to learn to do these jobs for themselves only to find that some 20 years later they had become recording engineers, web designers, road managers, live sound engineers and so on. This is not necessarily a bad thing—I myself set out at an early age to become a successful recording and touring artist but got caught up in producing and recording in the studio and happily, I am still there today.

COACH'S CORNER: Keeping an Open Mind

Often in life, the path to success in any endeavor is fraught with detours. You may think a straight line exists between your career desires and "living your dream," but often there are many side careers you will likely explore before achieving your ultimate objective.

Keep an open mind about the opportunities that may present themselves and be prepared for a variety of them. That means read LOTS of books and if you're going to school, study MANY subjects while you're there. This will increase your chances of being lucky. Your career might be like mine—always moving forward, but hardly moving in a straight line!

An important point to mention here is the clear distinction between those job titles that relate directly to music creation and those that revolve around the business of music. There's a strong delineation between these jobs that brings up an important set of self assessment questions that can help you better determine which side of the coin you are best suited for—the music or the business? Or perhaps both?

Self-Assessment Questions—Answer True or False
To determine where you might best belong in the music business, take a moment to seriously answer the following.

1. I enjoy working with computers and find myself drawn to discovering new creative software tools.
2. I am always hungry for information about new technologies and their potential impact on the entertainment industry.
3. I'm always the one who wires the home entertainment system and troubleshoots it when it's not working.
4. I spend hours playing with a new software program and amusing myself with pushing the envelopes of its capabilities.
5. I always embrace and am never scared by new ways of being creative.

Self-Assessment Questions continued

6. I'm a great "people person" and generally get along with most people.
7. I'm good at listening to other people's problems.
8. I am a good negotiator and always work to find compromises in difficult situations.
9. I'm a good communicator, even with people who others say are difficult.
10. I can keep my cool even under moments of conflict and extreme duress.

If you answered questions one through five as "true" four or more times, then you are most likely suited for a technical career in music. If you answered questions six through ten "true" four or more times, then you have a high chance of being well suited for the business side of the industry. If you answered "true" to eight or more of all ten questions, then you may very well be suited for entrepreneurship.

At the beginning of my "Planning for Success" classes, I always ask my students to complete a "Vision Statement" questionnaire—the purpose of which is to create a mental visualization of who you want to become and how you will map out the road to your ultimate goals and personal fulfillment. This can help you be able to predict the skills, responsibilities and future prospects of your chosen career path—even if the path goes forward and not straight!

Before creating this vision statement, one must first understand the careers of those who have come before you. With so many stunning success stories, there is much to be learned by reading about the careers of others you admire and respect. There are many published biographies and books composed of revealing, informative and amusing interviews with the behind the scenes luminaries of our times, including:

☛ *Making Records: The Scenes Behind the Music*, by engineering and producing giant Phil Ramone

☛ *Losing My Virginity*, by industry mogul Richard Branson of Virgin Records

☛ *The Operator*, by Geffen Records mastermind David Geffen

☛ *Behind the Glass*, by Howard Massey (with interviews, practical tips, artistic insights, and inside stories from pros behind the music like Daniel Lanois, T-Bone Burnett, Hugh Padgham and many more)

☛ *Mix Masters*, by Maureen Droney

☛ *Inside Tracks,* by Richard Buskin

☛ *The Art of Digital Music,* by Kelly Richards and David Battino

☛ *Masters of Music*, by Mark Small and Andrew Taylor, also features interviews but with a wide range of artists who talk in great detail about climbing the latter of success and attaining stardom.

A great place to start getting yourself steeped in the jargon and tools of the trade are the many industry trade magazines and their related web portals. Just as the music industry is being forced to evolve with the many changes in technology, so too is the print industry—many long-standing trade related magazines are becoming web-based information and content portals only. If anything, we will look back on the first decade of this millennium as the time when Web-centric business models took over practically all aspects of both the music and print industries!

A perfect example of the transition from print to web is the DJ-centric *Remix* magazine that has stopped being printed to become a web only e-zine (as of 2009). Penton Media publishes *Mix*, *Electronic Musician*, and *Remix*, and each can be found on the Web:

☛ www.mixonline.com,

☛ www.remixmag.com, and

☛ www.emusician.com

These "zines" are long known for insightful and up to date industry trends and interviews exploring the artists, the studios and the gear and applications behind the music.

Other helpful publications that explore the many facets of recording technology include: *EQ, Keyboard, Tape Op* and *Pro Sound News,* each (of course) with a Website. I have found these to be a very strong base of knowledge and I continue to read all of them to make sure I stay on top of industry trends. Each of their respective Websites has become a centerpiece of their new media business models. These resources are fantastic for gauging the trends of the industry, which can ultimately lead to opportunity and of course, jobs.

Jobs in the Music Business

So what kinds of jobs are there in the music business? The traditional recording studio is only one of many places to think about looking for a career. Most entry-level positions have many people calling, writing and often just showing up to get the gig—they're willing to do "anything" just to get their foot in the door. Don't let this competition discourage you. If you are diligent and honest with yourself about how deep your passion runs, you *will* find a job that best suits your skills and growth needs.

As of this writing, you should be aware that the advent of affordable digital audio technology, and the tremendous growth in computing power has created a significant decline in the large format-recording studio business. Essentially, recording studios are having a tougher time selling access to their studios to clients. This translates to fewer clients, lower rates and less job opportunities for you.

However, this does not mean there aren't studio jobs to be had. This decline has presented new opportunities for budding young engineers and would-be "*entre-producers*," (a term I use for music and sound producers with a penchant for freelance employment and entrepreneurship). While getting that "staff gig" is less likely, the studios themselves are always looking for producers and acts to record. A hungry entre-producer who seeks and finds acts to record can easily translate an employee role into a client role. Who do you think gets treated better at the studio, anyway?

There are many niches in the music industry so you may be thinking to yourself that your objective was simply to work in the "industry" and not to be a performer or recording artist. That is a perfectly acceptable position to have, as there are many talented people who make a great living helping others realize *their* creative visions. Regardless of the position you aspire to, you will never escape the need to promote and sell *yourself* as a valuable resource to those who will need your services. You will also be required to equip yourself with the many different skill sets that encompass many of these jobs.

Below is a breakdown of many traditional opportunities one can find in the world of music and audio production, divided into technical and administrative categories. For evaluation purposes, these begin with entry-level positions and work their way up. Included is also a salary base to help you better in assessing the playing field. Salary bases have been averaged and generally represent starting pay. You might find your local market to be priced higher or lower than these rates, but at least you have a guide to begin your search for a career based on salary potential.

Some Useful Information Sources

- *All You Need to Know About the Music Business,* by Donald S. Passman

- *Music Business Handbook & Career Guide,* by David Baskerville

- www.entertainment.howstuffworks.com/publicist1.htm

- www.mypursuit.com/careers-27-3043.05/Songwriter. html

- www.indeed.com (salary info)

- www.simplyhired.com (salary info)

Industry Jobs: Studio-Related Technical Positions

Intern: An internship is basically a trade—you give your time and efforts and the "employer" gives you training (but not always money). Most studios maintain some form of internship program. Depending on the size of the facility, interns will be asked to do a broad array of tasks including making coffee, running errands, answering phones, light office work (filing), organizing sound libraries, and if you're lucky—assisting the second or first engineer on sessions. (See **Figure 1**) Entry-level positions like these can be invaluable for those seeking to get their feet wet and earn some on-the-job experience. Beware that most internships are unpaid but can be used for earning class credits while in school. Certain local employment laws restrict employers from "hiring" unpaid interns unless they are currently in school and receiving class credits. Many companies bypass this by paying interns minimum wage. Internships can vary in employment length and duration and can be as comprehensive as full-time or as little as one day a week. Generally internships should last no longer than three to four months—open-ended internships can leave you open to being taken advantage of, where you become a servant to the studio with no chance of being hired.

The intern is the most likely entry point for many of you coming into this business, so here's a bit of information about what you should expect to do for someone as an intern. In this case, you're the studio intern.

Typical Job Description for a Studio Intern

General Responsibilities
• Assist and support Studio Manager and Asst. Facility Manager
• Maintain cleanliness and order throughout facilities and outside areas,
• Keep the lobby/breakroom presentable
• Arranging chairs back in place after a session
• Replacing light bulbs when needed
• Light cleaning in breakroom during and after sessions
* Work with second engineer to prepare for and/or assist with sessions when necessary

Maintenance Duties
• Exterior—cleaning up the tags, weeds, and trash outside
• Keeping studios clean: Throw out garbage on the desks, dishes back into sink, cables and equipment back into the workroom. Keep control rooms stocked with pens, paper, clipboard, Sharpies, and pencils.

Work Room Organization
Make sure tools, gear, and cables are put back into workroom, ready for its next use. Maintain/update inventory of iLoks, dongles, mics, cables, etc. Keep workroom organized and clean.

Figure 1: *Typical job description for a studio intern.*

Assistant Engineer: The assistant is there to support the first engineer by performing tasks that would normally take the first engineer away from the flow of the session, from running cables to mic setups to headphone mixes to running for lunch and cleaning up after every session. The position of 'the second' is very valuable to those wanting to learn from the seasoned expertise of the first engineer as they will be trusted with extremely important tasks that require focus on details such as: documenting all session data, archiving of digital audio workstation session files, uploading mixes for band/producer/client review, making sure that session data is secure (no files prematurely leaked to the Internet before the album release date!) and dutifully backed up. Assistants often work closely with clients, which makes the difference between a great studio experience and an average one. Starting pay can range from $10 to $20/hr.

Maintenance Engineer: There was a time when having an in-house maintenance engineer was a requirement, but smaller facilities will often have a second engineer or studio manager who's capable of handling basic-level maintenance chores. There may be some vintage pieces of gear that need attention as well as a network of computers, hard drives and software that need constant maintenance and updates. This is where the role of maintenance engineer will cross over into the domain of information technology (IT). Today's maintenance engineer must know a good deal about computers and their related software/hardware systems as much as they need to know audio gear. These skills are highly sought after and having them virtually guarantees employment potential. In fact, many seasoned maintenance engineers have gone on to start their own companies, offering maintenance contracts to smaller studios that can't afford to keep a full-time maintenance engineer on staff! In most major markets, entry-level salaries are in the range of $45,000 to $50,000 per year.

First Engineer: First engineers are the seasoned veterans who've already worked on numerous recordings and find themselves in the enviable position of being in demand. First engineers may well have a "sound" that certain artists are looking for or at least a track record that proves they can create pro-sounding recordings. First engineers can be divided into two categories: tracking engineers and mixing engineers, although many do both. Knowing the studio and all of its many applications is only a starting point to being a good first engineer—the other half of the job is knowing how to work with people (both clients and artists). Managing client expectations is also very important. Younger artists and producers are often unaware of the large amount of time involved in recording, which can result in "sticker shock:" when the bill comes due. The engineer must be prepared to gauge the level of expectation and carefully communicate so artists understand the limitations of their budgets and how best to use their time in the studio. First engineer salaries can range broadly depending on the client base, the number of hits and reputation. Salaries generally begin at $50,000 to $60,000 per year, with raises marked by the success of the recordings and projects being produced.

Mastering Engineer: As defined by Wikipedia,

"A mastering engineer is one skilled in the practice of taking audio (typically musical content) that has been previously mixed in either the analog or digital domain as mono, stereo, or multichannel formats and prepares it for use in distribution, whether by physical media such as a CD, vinyl record, or as some method of streaming audio."

According to Michael Romanowski, a well-known SF mastering engineer, (www.michaelromanowskimastering.com), Pyramind Studio partner and NARAS member,

"Mastering is the tail end of the creative production process and the beginning of the manufacturing production process."

This specialized form of engineering requires not only a deep understanding of the tools required for the trade but also record production skills that allow them to troubleshoot mix issues and effectively help improve the sound of the final product. This job also requires an understanding of all the various delivery formats and their accompanying documentation requirements. Mastering studios are specialized environments using expensive analog and digital processors dedicated to the process of mastering audio recordings. Many studios today offer mastering services using software plug-ins designed to approximate the results of the more expensive outboard equipment used by the dedicated mastering studio. The quality of the results varies according to the algorithm these programs use to operate and the skill of the engineer. Many mastering engineers earn hourly ranges from $75 to $200 per hour (or more!) and often own the mastering studio.

Music Producer: Producers come in many flavors—those who become very involved in the songwriting and arranging, others who are more technical in their approach and many that refuse to be involved in the engineering process—other than to voice their objection when something doesn't "sound right." Regardless, the successful producer is *often* a music industry veteran who's comfortable behind a mix desk and negotiating contracts. To be a good producer, one needs to have a complete understanding of the recording process as well as strong communication and organizational skills. In the music industry the producer will often act as the go-between the artist, the studio and the label, if there is one. Being trusted enough to hold this position by the artist and the label requires a track record of success. To do so, you will have to be passionate and doggedly determined to produce as many projects as you possibly can, establishing a track record of successful projects.

At the beginning you may have to take on projects that may not be as personally satisfying as you would have hoped, but experience here is worth more than any education could ever afford. Salary and pay scale can vary widely, with young producers generally charging anywhere from $20 to $35 per hour and seasoned veterans charging as much as $75 per hour or more. Hourly rates will vary greatly based on what the producer brings to the party. Very often producers will have their own specialized equipment set and will offer to take the project to their own private studio for editing or even tracking or mixing. In this case, hourly rates don't always apply—producers can charge by the song or by the record, which takes the pressure off of watching the clock, making the artist more comfortable and able to perform at their best. Producers can also negotiate for royalties based on their name and clout in the industry as well as their ability to "spec" studio time based on deferred or back-end payments. In short, producers take on more financial risk with the project but often earn more reward when a record sells well. Engineers are less likely to earn this sort of back-end royalty, so they often get higher hourly rates.

Re-recording Mixer: In a film or video project, the re-recording mixer prepares the separate elements from the music, effects and dialog (whether as individual discrete tracks or premixed into multichannel "stems" and mixes these tracks to create the project's final mix. A re-recording mixer may work in solo or as a member of a team of re-recording mixers on a complex project. During the production process, they also have the responsibility of creating temporary mixes used by the composer, music editor, picture editor or director during different phases as the project progresses. During the mixes, re-recording mixers also add ambience and or equalization to the tracks, set up panning or spatial cues, and may have to create multiple mixes for various release formats (i.e., mono, stereo, LCRS and/or 5.1/6.1/7.1 surround), depending on the production needs. Pay can vary widely, as many re-recording mixers works on a per-project basis.

ADR Mixer: Also known as looping, ADR stands for automated dialog replacement, although ironically, there's nothing automatic about it. The ADR mixer is the person who re-records dialog in the studio, simulating the location recorded sound and making sure that all the dialog on film soundtracks is accurately placed, and of the best possible quality. On big budget films, this job may be split into several paid positions. On medium-to-low budget films, the work will be outsourced to a smaller post-production house, where one person will put in very long hours to ensure that the work gets done. ADR mixers will insure that any dialog must be replaced due to mispronunciation, replacement of adult language for TV broadcasts or unintelligible delivery. ADR mixers will also be involved in the dubbing process, which refers to recorded voices that do not belong to the original actors and speak a different language from the one the actor originally spoke. The national average annual salary for ADR mixers is about $35,000. In larger media markets, this can range from $45,000 to $75,000.

Location Recordist: The location recordist is the engineer who captures the sound on set. While dialog is the most important thing to record on set, the location recordist might also capture complex, low-level, ambient noise (aka room tone). The need for quiet on-set recordings have pushed the technical limits of modern recording equipment, which now boast lower noise floors and extended frequency response in a portable system. Depending on the size of the production, this position might be referred to as boom operator or field recordist. The average annual income is about $55,000.

Video Game Sound Implementation: Sound implementation involves the use of middleware, which is software designed to interface with other software, i.e., game engines. Middlewares such as FMOD and Wwise bring music, sound effects, and mix attributes into the game engine. A music and sound implementation specialist is ultimately responsible for the interactive nature of the audio in a game.

Theme Park Audio Technician: Music is an incredibly important part of theme parks. Disney World's EPCOT Center, for example, focuses on sharing culture from dozens of countries around the world through entertainment with music as an integral part of the experience. There is music going on at all times with nightly parades comprised of marching bands, professional ensembles as well as student bands from all over the country get the opportunity to perform in front of the thousands of theme park patrons and live shows at almost all times using both live and canned sound. Not only is there music happening in almost every section of these theme parks, voice-over recordings are used for kiosks, transportation services, and loudspeaker introduction to parades and live events, all of which are updated periodically to achieve a contemporary sound. There are dozens of amphitheaters and auditoriums and in each location there is an engineer operating the sound equipment to make sure that everything runs smoothly. Some performances are entirely previously recorded audio and some are a mixture of live dialog from the stage actors and canned music from a digital source.

Industry Jobs—Studio-Related Administrative Positions

Studio Scheduler: Scheduling studio time is never as easy as it may seem. Each session has its own technical requirements, which necessitate an experienced individual who can not only decipher these requirements but also match them up with the right control room(s) and the right engineer. Typical questions that a scheduler might have to ask include:

☛ What kind of session is it?

☛ Is it a tracking session, overdub, mixing or mastering?

☛ How many pieces and what instrumentation will be recorded?

☛ Are there any specialty pieces of equipment that will be required, such as microphones, preamps, musical instruments, software, outboard gear, etc.?

☛ Will the client be working with picture (film/video) and what format?

The list is endless and requires a detailed understanding of the capabilities of the studio and its staff. Often a good scheduler will also be a second engineer or even the studio manager. Studio scheduler salaries can range from $20 per hour to an annual salary of $30,000 to $40,000 dollars. This will depend on how versatile you are and what other roles you fulfill!

Studio Manager: The studio manager (in smaller facilities, often the owner and/or first engineer) plays a critical role in the day-to-day operations of the studio as well as acting as the studio salesperson. (see **Figure 2**) They work closely with the studio owner to maintain profitable operations, work directly with clients to create attractive studio time offerings as well as working on the more complicated requests for proposals (RFPs). Often studio managers will work on salary plus commission, which depend greatly on their savvy and experience level. (More clients equal more commissions. Starting salaries range from $30,000 to $50,000 dollars per year depending on your pre-existing client base and industry contacts.

Typical Job Description for a Studio Manager

General Responsibilities
• Book sessions for studio clientele, utilizing and managing studio resources (equipment and personnel) for such sessions
• Create promotional materials and concepts to grow production business
• Find clients to record and/or mix/master
• Develop intern program and train interns to support studio management and engineering needs
• Open facilities Monday through Friday at 9 AM
• Maintain daily morning walkthrough of facilities to assure general cleanliness and presentation of studio
• Manage and schedule engineering, mixing and mastering staff, and consultants for all bookings
• As executive assistant, handle light administrative duties, including filing, general office organization, mailings, daily outgoing mail, and coordinate bill payment with accounting
• Manage invoicing and on-spot payment for studio sessions
• Report to executive director on a monthly basis regarding development of studio clientele
• Determining what mics/pres/gear are available and check functionality of everything
• Account for gear and monitor for all gear being checked out by staff.
• Make recommendations on gear studio has available or needs to procure
• Create rate schedules for tracking, mix, and mastering sessions
• Work with marketing coordinator to plan and manage event requirements

Examples of Possible Goals
• Bring in voiceover business and music clientele to increase production services revenue by 20 percent
• Expand studio services scheduling and staff to be available for 24/7 operation

Figure 2: *Typical job description for a studio manager.*

Sound Supervisor: The sound supervisor oversees the sound post-production process of film or television programs. The sound supervisor will work closely with the director to accomplish the artistic and storytelling goals of the film, which requires coordinating and managing all of the sound work to be done.

While this person will have the final say on the sound editing, they most likely will not do all the work. They will be responsible for budgeting, scheduling, as well as audio crisis management. As of July, 2009 the average salary for the U.S. was about $55,000. In places such as New York and Los Angeles, the average is $20,000 to $30,000 more. With more credits by one's name and reputation in the industry, a sound supervisor will earn a significantly higher than average income.

Music Supervisor: The music supervisor is the member of the production team upon whom the responsibility of securing the right to use any copyrighted musical content in a film or television production falls. This person may also supervise the composition of the original score. The music supervisor chooses appropriate music for a given scene, especially source cues (music that is actually in the scene with the characters, i.e., on the car radio or on a home stereo) and songs. This is generally a per-project job, with compensation ranging from a few hundred dollars per television episode, to between $20,000 and $200,000 per film, with an average annual salary of $51,000.

Licensing Manager: A licensing manager works for a label, distributor or anyone managing a large catalog of music that either owns the publishing rights or has an administration contract to license the music. Music licensing deals have become an extremely important source of revenue for artists, songwriters and their affiliate labels. Licensing managers spend many hours on the phone and in meetings working to secure placement for the catalog of music they represent in any of the following: films, television shows, commercials, Websites, games, and mobile media. Salaries can vary greatly depending on the size and caliber of the library being represented as well as bonus structures based on successful placement.

Business Manager: The business manager is responsible for the handling of a client's money. They collect and keep track of it, file taxes, pay bills, invest the money, etc. Business managers are generally college educated in finance, and many are Certified Public Accountants. Though their primary focus will be money, in the entertainment industry this can amount to dealing with a wide range of issues. This person might be involved in: projecting budgets and forecasting income; coordinating wills and overseeing the client's estate; monitoring insurance needs; even overseeing divorces. A business manager likely has a written agreement that defines in detail what his or her responsibilities are—and are not! Business managers must have effective communication skills in order to explain financial situations to the client but ultimately the client should be making the decisions. It is, however, the business manager's ethical duty to help educate the client as to what the best decision might be but many who are put in this position take advantage of their clients and get rich at their expense. Payment varies from client to client, depending on the circumstances. Earnings may come in the form of a percentage (five percent is common), flat fee, hourly rate, or some combination. The median annual income for entertainment business managers in 2004 was $60,000.

Publicist: The job of the music publicist is to perpetuate positive press coverage for the client/artist. To best accomplish this goal, publicists will build and maintain professional relationships with industry journalists by sending them timely, newsworthy story ideas that are original and related to the client. Press releases are a great way to spread "the news" in a simple uniform message to many media outlets at once. Publicists cultivate these relationships by spending time after the workday has ended to befriend those reporters, editors, and TV news producers. This profession is almost entirely dependent on networking skills with much of the publicist's day spent on the phone and corresponding via e-mail. While there will inevitably be some negative press around an artist or an album, if the publicist has been good to the media, the media might be kinder to the client. An average salary for a publicist is around $46,500 a year but can soar into the stratosphere depending on the size and caliber of a publicist's clientele and whether or not they are working for themselves or a PR firm.

Music Journalist: Music journalists write for various publications including newspapers, magazines, various Internet entities or one television network or another. Some journalists will exclusively write reviews and often gain free entry to concert events and receive new releases for free, in exchange for the press coverage. Other journalists will cover artists in depth via direct interviews with the artists and with people close to the artist. This allows them to paint a broad picture of a certain period of an artists life, and information that might otherwise be unreleased to the public can be ascertained by a good journalist—all of which make for great biographies as well! To be a music journalist, one should have a degree in journalism or communications, although naturally gifted writers who absolutely love music could carry themselves to the top of this industry. Music journalism is a field in which people skills are mandatory—perhaps more so than any other aspect of the industry.

Music Educator: The incorporation of musical training from an early age is common in most nations, because involvement in music is considered a fundamental component of human behavior and virtually all human cultures, each possessing its own musical language that reflects its traditions, concerns, and activities. Music educators, through a combination of set curriculum and methodology of instruction, impart their knowledge of music theory, history, instrumentality, and/or general wisdom to students who want to learn, whether taught privately or as a part of a larger institution. Elementary school music teachers earn about $42,000 a year. The average is about $36,000 a year at the high school level. At the university level, the annual average is about $39,000 while private instructors at some institutions can earn much more.

Industry Jobs—Studio-Related Creative Positions

Work for Hire Composer: A work for hire composer is someone who is paid a flat fee for the composition of a piece or segment of music for: film, advertising, television, video games, industrials or remixes. The main tasks of the work for hire composer is composing and arranging the music. This is now commonly done using computer-based MIDI sequencing and digital orchestration sound libraries. To succeed, one must have a healthy knowledge of both music creation software and music theory as well as be familiar with many styles of music. Also important is the ability to deliver what the client is looking for in a timely fashion, so being able to take directions effectively is essential. Works for hire agreements can vary dramatically in price and will depend on the industry recognition of the composer and the scope of work. Traditionally, the composer of a piece of music is the exclusive copyright owner of that work once it has been set in a *fixed form*—meaning written as sheet music or a physical/digital audio recording. Depending on the nature of the agreements, composers may or may not retain their share of the writer's copyright. All rights as they pertain to publishing and/or licensing will be owned by the entity commissioning the work.

Sound Designer: Generally considered a hybrid of technical and creative, the sound designer creates the signature sound-scape of a film, video game, theatrical performance or any moving picture requiring more than music and dialog. The sound designer develops textures, ambiences and effects that support the musical score and help to create a mood for the visual image. Sound designers can be awarded an Oscar or a Tony Award for achieving excellence in motion picture film and on Broadway. They are a very integral part to the creation of animated films and video games. Sound designers can work either in-house with a production company or studio or as independent contractors. Salaries can range dramatically based on the caliber of work and clients.

Foley Artist: The Foley artist is the person who creates many of the natural sound effects in a film. These sound effects are recorded in a studio with a recording engineer during post-production. Often the case may be that the microphone didn't pick up the sound effects that occurred naturally during the filming of a scene, or for other reasons are unusable. The case may also be that there is no sound recorded on-location, and all the sounds need to be added by the Foley artist and sound designer. Foley artists might also exaggerate existing sounds. Many take great pride in their sound effects apparatuses, often using common household items to make uncommon movie sounds. Foley is named for Jack Foley who pioneered the art form in the early days of pictures with sound. The average annual salary for a Foley artist is around $55,000.

Music Editor: The music editor is an audio engineer who works with the composer, director and other creative entities to organize the music cues for a project. They work closely with the composer in the early stages to keep track of all decisions made by the director pertaining to placement, timing, length, and type of music, which will be used throughout the project. The music editor will generally be the person engineering the recording sessions, keeping track of cues and generating the click (if necessary) to ensure precise timing of recorded music. They are also present during sessions where the music is actually inserted into the project, making sure that precise time code placement occurs. A music editor's salary is around $68,000.

Songwriter: A songwriter is someone who works individually, or in a team of two or more people to write songs. Songwriters can be hired by any type of organization to write in any style of music—from an opera to a pop song. They generally play at least one instrument and have done so for most of their lives and have likely studied music theory, as well as other songwriters/composer's works. Many songwriters will perform their own pieces—such as Bob Dylan or John Mayer—while others might write with the goal of licensing their music to other more well-known artists for a fee and a chance to earn significant publishing and performance royalties should the song become popular. Earnings for songwriters will vary dramatically and it is difficult to judge an average salary. According to research presented at Mypursuit.com, in 2006, it was estimated at $40,000, but of this group the middle half made anywhere from $23,600 to $60,400, with the lowest 10% making less than $15,200. The highest 10% of this group made more than $110,900.

Instrumentalist: An instrumentalist is a professional musician. While this is the goal of many musicians, to make it a sole source of income is a feat accomplished by a relatively small number of people. Many instrumentalists supplement their income by teaching and have another job that may or may not be related to music—many sell musical equipment for example. A studio musician will play for a studio recording of an album or single song while a live instrumentalist may have a regular gig at a club, or go on tour in support of an album. Being an instrumentalist often means extensive traveling, which makes it hard to really call somewhere home. Younger artists tend to enjoy this lifestyle but as time goes on it can wear on the soul. Older musicians, unless they are name recognizable brands might not feel it is worth the trouble of touring. Musicians set aside many hours daily for practice, as polished skills and an expansive repertoire are requirements to achieve and maintain a professional level of musicianship. The average annual income (not supplemented) for instrumentalists is around $18,000.

Arranger: An arranger is someone who rewrites some or all parts of a previously written composition, often by substituting chords in the progression or enhancing the instrumentation. This process might be done to modernize an old classic, or to present a piece in a different style. It can also be as simple as changing the key for a vocalist whose range might not reach all the notes of the melody in the current arrangement. The arranger often works alongside a songwriter to help finish a piece of music. A songwriter may have several parts of a song but hit a roadblock trying to put the pieces together. Arrangers are usually "work for hire" but may also work as part of a songwriting team. The average annual income for a music arranger is between $40k to $42k.

Copyist: A music copyist is someone who copies down notation and puts together a chart or score for a band/orchestra or publication. Copyists must have extensive knowledge in multiple styles and understand notational conventions, so that the piece of written music makes sense to those reading it. Until the 1990s, this was done by hand with a calligraphy pen, manuscript paper, and a ruler. With the advent of notation software such as Finale and Sibelius, as well as built in scoring features available in modern DAWs such as Apple Computer's Logic and Digidesign's Pro Tools, hand-written scores are becoming a lost art form.

Video Game Audio Director: The audio director is the person providing guidance, maintaining creative direction of audio, and keeping everyone on schedule and on budget in the production of the audio for a video game. Responsibilities of this position include providing creative vision for the sound department, managing schedules for multiple simultaneously occurring projects, communicating with the production team about the requirements, processes, and status of the a specific project, keeping the audio department at the forefront of technology and game audio trends, ordering new equipment and ensuring the proper development of proprietary tools and audio-engine features that make the game experience unique. This position requires significant experience with game audio along with leadership and management experience. A foundation of technical audio theory, as well as knowledge of scripting and/or programming and knowledge of current and next-gen gaming console audio capabilities is also required. Audio directors often have an undergrad degree in a related field such as music or engineering. The average annual salary for a video game audio director is about $85,000 but can vary greatly depending on the size of the game company and their bonus and benefits structure.

Video Game Music Director: For a video game, the music director is the person who decides what music is selected and when it gets used in a game. They spend time researching genres, artists, attitudes and lifestyles to make sure that the music and gameplay match up. They decide when and where to used licensed musical content versus original composition, set the budgets and are often very involved in negotiating the deals with both original score composers and artists whose music is being licensed. The average annual salary for a video game music director is about $65,000 but can vary greatly depending on the size of the game company and their bonus and benefits structure.

Personal Vision Statements

Now that you've learned a bit about some types of jobs in the music production industry, this is a good time to complete your vision statement and answer the fundamental questions that will guide you in finding your career path. It is extremely important that you be honest and critical in evaluating both your skill sets and talents but also to be gentle enough with yourself to allow for growth and training to help get you the rest of the way there.

This should be considered a living document—one that you come back to and evaluate and update regularly. It's always fun to see how your perspective changes over time and how your experiences and training affects your decision-making process. The questions in the vision statement are designed to help you evaluate your desires as well as the realities and consequential effects that the pursuit of those desires may bring.

I've provided space here for you to answer these questions within these pages, but many people copy them to new pages and answer them there. They collect the answers and keep them as a first draft of their careers. Feel free to do this digitally too!

Use both your research and personal skills and talent assessment to help you answer the following questions:

1. Do you see yourself as a self-starter or someone who works best with leadership and guidance?

2. What attracts you to the music and sound industry?

3. What do you see as your top three talents?

4. What are your top three interests in the music and sound industry?

5. What job descriptions match up with your top three interests outlined in question #3?

6. How much money do you think you can earn for each of the above job descriptions?

    _____

7. Where do you see yourself in the next three, five, and ten years?

    _____

8. If you were to start your own business in the music and sound industry, describe what that would be, in one brief paragraph.

9. How much money do you think you would earn in this business? How much money do you think you would need to start the business?

10. List three job experiences that gave you the most satisfaction.

11. List three job experiences that gave you the least satisfaction.

12. Pick the number one company you would like to work for today and write a paragraph explaining why you should be the one chosen for your dream opportunity.

13. What is the single most important thing you hope to gain from a career in the music and sound industry?

Question #1 ("Do you see yourself as a self-starter or someone who works best with leadership and guidance?") is designed to make you think about the difference between entrepreneurship and employment and asks you which you feel you are more suited for.

Question #2 ("What attracts you to the music and sound industry?") attempts to begin to narrow down your decision making process by evaluating what it is about the industry that is drawing you in.

Question #3 ("What do you see as your top three talents?") forces you to self assess yourself. Which of these talents if any are relevant to question number two?

Question #4 ("What are your top three interests in the music and sound industry") helps you evaluate your top interests helping you further hone in on what will make your career path meaningful and fulfilling.

Question #5 ("What job descriptions match up with your top three interests outlined in question #3?") forces you to apply your research to practical jobs that will apply to both your skill sets and your interests.

Question #6 (" How much money do you think you can earn for each of the above job descriptions?) is a reality check, making sure that whatever career path you choose will match up with your cost of living and need for material gain.

Question #7 ("Where do you see yourself in the next three, five, and ten years?") requires you to place a timeline on your vision. After all, time waits for no one and my experience shows that more results happen when you place a timeline on them!

Question #8 ("If you were to start your own business in the music and sound industry, what that would be?") is a direct challenge to the entrepreneur in all of us. Entrepreneurship is not for everyone but by writing down your vision for a business you begin to explore what that looks like and will see if this holds any fire for you. Same goes for question nine.

Questions #9 and #10 ("How much money do you think you would earn in this business? How much money do you think you would need to start the business?; and "List three job experiences that gave you the *most* satisfaction.") ask that you look at what it is that does and doesn't bring you satisfaction in the work place (leave money out of this one!).

Question #11 ("List three job experiences that gave you the *least* satisfaction.") will help you to be clear about what you don't like. What not to pursue is just as important as being clear about what you do like and what you want to pursue.

Question #12 ("Pick the number one company you would like to work for today and explain why you should be the one chosen for your dream opportunity.") helps you focus your career goals by singling out which company in your mind aligns itself the most with your vision of success.

Question #13 ("What is the single most important thing you hope to gain from a career in the music and sound industry?") hopefully proves that you have much more at stake here than monetary gain!

Useful Resources for Achieving Success

Professional Organizations to Support Your Career

The National Academy Of Recording Arts and Sciences
The Recording Academy® has twelve chapters spread out across the United States and represents the interests of thousands of musicians, producers, recording engineers and other recording professionals. Its stated mission is to improve the quality of life and cultural condition for music and its makers.

Membership to the Recording Academy comes in several different forms. To be a voting member one must have at least six credits on commercially released recordings distributed in retail stores or at least ten credits on songs being digitally distributed by sites other than your own. Associate members are non-voting but can equally engage in Recording Academy events and can even be eligible to sit on the various Boards. Both voting and associate memberships are $100 annually. Students currently in college or a related music industry vocational school can qualify for a dramatically discounted membership of $25 per year.

Membership brings with it the distinct privilege of allowing you to create a profile page on the Grammy365 web site. This site was designed for members only and allows you to network and make direct contacts with the 20,000 other members of the Academy nationwide. It's a lot like Facebook; allowing you to upload and share music, video, and product and location reviews, but for Academy members only!

The National headquarters for The Recording Academy is in Los Angeles California with its other eleven chapters being in San Francisco, Seattle, Nashville, Chicago, New York, Washington DC, Miami, Atlanta, Philadelphia, Austin, and Memphis. If you live or work in any of these cities one of the best places to begin is with a visit to your local chapter office. Chapter offices represent the Academy on a local level by working within that region's music and recording communities and addressing its needs through education, advocacy, professional development and events. Most important to all of this is the chapter's ability to act as a hub for members to meet, network and address the concerns of the recording industry both nationally and locally.

COACH'S CORNER: You and The Recording Academy

The music industry is made up of many interesting characters and networks of professionals and one the largest such networks is represented by the organization whose voting members annually select the recipients of the time honored Grammy® Awards. This however, is only the most commercialized center point of an organization that seeks to do so much to better the lives of those seeking to make a living in the music business. The Recording Academy is a non-profit organization that encompasses numerous arms including the Grammy Foundation, MusiCares, Grammy U, The Producers & Engineers Wing, and The Grammy Museum.

The Chapters are run by a small staff (two to three usually, including an executive director, a production coordinator, an assistant and often an intern) and are governed by a volunteer board of governors that have elected officers and trustees. The officers and trustees make up the executive committee who in conjunction with the staff executive director responsible for the financial health and stewardship of the chapter.

Each board of every chapter is composed of numerous committees that seek to further the interests of the chapters. It is here where much of the community-based work gets done and it is also here where anyone interested and willing to roll up their sleeves and get involved can have a lot of impact. Committees can range from the all-encompassing Education Committee to genre-driven music committees like Urban or Indie Rock.

The Producers & Engineers Wing of the Academy guides the committee most focused on the interests of both engineers and producers. Commonly referred to as the P&E Wing, this division of the Academy is comprised of more than 5,500 producers, engineers, remixers, manufacturers, technologists, and other related music recording industry professionals.

As a national membership initiative of The Recording Academy, the P&E Wing provides a vehicle to reach a specific constituency, to craft advocacy positions, and to better address the daily concerns of these individuals. Among these issues are the development and adoption of new technologies; recommendations for best practices in recording, master delivery, archiving and preservation, and support for both music education and education in the recording arts. Primary to the P&E Wings initiatives is increasing awareness of the value of the art and craft of recording and to work with the Academy's advocacy department to promote the rights of creative professionals in the areas of intellectual property, new streams of revenue, music preservation, music education, and freedom of expression.

Detailed information on current events and initiatives by the P&E Wing and many of the different committees can be found at www.grammy.com and the new www.grammy365.com site, which seeks to bring the recording academy into the age of social networking, blogging, and user content driven support.

There are many organizations that seek to help their communities through education and networking opportunities. But very few, if any, have succeeded in galvanizing the greater recording community of the United States in working together to bring our cause and make our needs and value evident to our congressmen and Senators in Washington D.C.

NARIP: Another organization that does a good job of helping educate its constituency as well as promote healthy networking opportunities is The National Association of Recording Industry Professionals, also known as NARIP. NARIP's founder, Tess Taylor, is an author and contributor to this book! Where The Recording Academy casts a very wide net, NARIP focuses on promoting education, career advancement, and good will among record company executives. NARIP offers professional development opportunities, educational programs and seminars and the opportunity to meet and interact with peers. It also has a job bank, a member résumé database for employers, and a mentor network. NARIP membership was created for, and is restricted to record industry professionals who work at a major or independent label, are record distributors, or work in or with record marketing or personal management firms.

Lawyers, publicists and consultants whose main client base is the record business are also welcome. Owned and operated by Tess Taylor, NARIP draws from its strong industry-driven base to present current and up to date panels and seminars on some of the most pressing issues facing the industry at any given time. The events are open to the public for a small fee and can also be purchased on DVD or audio CD via its Website: www.narip.com

There are many international and regional organizations worth looking into. Thought must be put into your specific industry niche and genre of music to be certain your time and effort with whichever organization you choose to affiliate with is appropriate.

American Federation of Musicians (AFM): With over 250 local unions throughout the United States and Canada, AFM (www .afm.org) is the largest union in the world representing the interests of the professional musician.

American Society of Composers, Authors & Publishers (ASCAP): With more than 370,000 U.S. composers, songwriters, lyricists, and music publishers, ASCAP (www.ascap.com) is a performing rights organization that licenses and distributes royalties for the non-dramatic public performances of their copyrighted works. ASCAP members represent every kind of music, including pop, rock, alternative, country, R&B, rap, hip-hop, Latin, film/television music, folk, roots and blues, jazz, gospel, Christian, new age, theater and cabaret, dance, electronic, symphonic, concert, and many others— the entire musical spectrum.

Association of Professional Recording Services (APRS): The APRS (www2.aprs.co.uk) membership includes recording studios, post-production houses, mastering, replication, pressing and duplicating facilities, and providers of education and training, as well as audio engineers, manufacturers, suppliers, and consultants. Its primary aim is to develop and maintain excellence at all levels within the audio industry of the United Kingdom.

Audio Engineering Society (AES): The Audio Engineering Society (www.aes.org) is the only professional society devoted exclusively to audio technology. Its membership is comprised of leading engineers, scientists and other authorities. The AES serves its members, the industry and the public by stimulating and facilitating advances in the constantly changing field of audio. It encourages and disseminates new developments through annual technical meetings and exhibitions of professional equipment, and through the *Journal of the Audio Engineering Society*, the professional archival publication in the audio industry.

Australian Record Industry Association (ARIA): The Australian Record Industry Association (www.aria.com.au) was established and operates to represent the broad interests of all member record companies. ARIA has more than 80 members, ranging from small "boutique" labels, to medium-size companies and very large companies employing thousands of people. ARIA acts as an advocate for the industry, domestically and internationally. ARIA also collects statistical information from members and retailers. It compiles numerous ARIA charts with data provided by over 700 retailers and more.

Broadcast Music, Inc. (BMI): Broadcast Music, Inc. (www.bmi.com) collects license fees on behalf of songwriters, composers and music publishers from businesses that use music and distributes them as royalties to those members whose works have been performed. This non-profit organization was founded in 1939 by radio executives to provide competition in the field of performing rights, to assure royalty payments to writers and publishers of music (such as blues, country, jazz, R&B, gospel, folk, Latin and—ultimately—rock and roll) that were then not represented by the existing performing right organization and provide an alternative source of licensing for all music users.

Electronic Music Foundation (EMF): The mission of EMF (www.emf.org) is to explore the creative and cultural potential in the convergence of music, sound, technology, and science, and, through contact and interactions with a large and growing public, apply what is learned towards the betterment of human life. EMF supports, promotes, and documents the work of 1,600 professional associates worldwide. It commissions innovative work, publishes and distributes CDs and DVDs, fosters research, develops collaborative projects with partners and contacts, and maintains Websites on the history and current practice of electronic music. EMF provides models and resources for creativity and communicates the development and exchange of new ideas throughout the world.

International Federation of the Phonographic Industry (IFPI): IFPI (www.ifpi.org) is the organization representing the international recording industry. It comprises a membership of 1,500 record producers and distributors in 76 countries, with national groups in 46 countries. IFPI's international secretariat is based in London and is linked to regional offices in Brussels, Hong Kong, Miami, and Moscow.

NAMM (International Music Products Association, formerly the National Association of Music Merchants): Founded in 1901, NAMM (www.namm.org) has been the engine driving the music products industry, enabling both large and small businesses to maximize productivity and reduce the costs of doing business. With more than 9,000 Members in the United States and 100+ other countries, NAMM is ultimately dedicated to expanding the market and giving people of all ages the opportunity to experience the proven benefits of making music.

Music Producers Guild (MPG): The United Kingdom-based Music Producers Guild (www.mpg.org.uk/home) represents the interests of U.K. record producers, music recording engineers, mixers, and anyone else directly involved in the production of recorded music. Additionally, the MPG has strong links to education and cutting-edge manufacturers of new technologies who all help shape tomorrow's standards and trends in today's sophisticated recording environment.

National Association of Recording Merchandisers (NARM): A not-for-profit trade association, NARM (www.narm.com) serves the music content delivery community in a variety of areas including networking, advocacy, information, education and promotion. NARM advances the promotion, marketing, distribution, and sale of music by providing its members with a forum for diverse meeting and networking opportunities, information, and education to support their businesses, as well as advocating for their common interests.

SESAC: Founded in 1930, SESAC (www.sesac.com) is the second oldest performing rights organization in the United States. SESAC's corporate headquarters in Nashville houses all of the company's divisions, from creative to licensing to administration. The company also has offices in New York, Los Angeles and London.

Society of Professional Audio Recording Services (SPARS): SPARS (www.spars.com) was founded in 1979 by the leaders of the recording industry. Its members enjoy the access and opportunity to network with some of the best known and most successful individuals in the business. In addition, the roster of SPARS past presidents reads like a Who's Who with regard to the history of recording. SPARS is an organization dedicated to sharing practical, "hands-on" business information about facility ownership, management and operations. The SPARS community includes audio recording and mastering facilities, manufacturers, engineers, and multimedia specialists—everything from single-operator studios to large multi-room facilities.

Women In Music The National Network for Women in Music (http://www.womeninmusic.com/) is a non-profit membership organization designed to promote the recognition of women in music through services, education, and networking resources. Founded in 1993, WIMNN provides a network to support research efforts and opportunities for women in music. Subscriptions, donations and sponsorships are used to support the organization's goals and objectives which include its Website, seminars, mentor programs, newsletter, and a variety of other educational and business activities.

Schmooze or Lose: Networking Tips

It should go without saying that good networking skills are extremely helpful when it comes to landing a job or running your own music industry related business. The old saying "it's who you know" still has a lot of mileage and is helpful in getting doors to open but in the end, it will always be your skills and experience that keep you there once you have crossed the threshold.

If you are starting from ground zero, the best approach is a combined effort of online social networking and your local industry offering networking and educational events. NARAS is a great example of this type of industry social hub, located in 12 major cities in the US. A portion of *every day* should be reserved to building and nurturing your network. One of the reasons this is such an important process is this: the best opportunities are rarely advertised. Industry people do not want to be swamped with résumés and cover letters that will require many time consuming hours to comb through to find the right candidate—they just want to turn to their network of trusted colleagues to seek out recommendations. Your objective is to become a part of as many of these networks as possible in order to find yourself in the proverbial right place at the right time!

Go to as many industry trade shows, seminars, and events—wherever and whenever possible. There are numerous annual events throughout the U.S. but there's no way to attend them all.

COACH'S CORNER: The "In-Person" Approach

I cannot stress enough the importance of your geographic location when it comes to networking! Even with the power of online social networking sites like Grammy365.com, Linkedin, Plaxos, Facebook, MySpace, etc., there is still no substitute for face-to-face interactions. Social Networking can be good for extensive résumé review and getting a sense of a person's background and experience, but it creates no meaningful connection anywhere close to the one you get with a handshake. The entertainment industry is very much a "people business" and there is nothing like "pressing the flesh" to make these connections come to life. This is not a business for the shy and introspective—you might be able to get away with that if you are a recording and performance artist for whom that works as a stage persona. But if you are a part of the 99 percent of the rest of us, you will need to put on your happy face and prepare yourself to be engaging and personable.

Focus on the biggest ones or the ones that relate most closely to your desired career. One of the oldest and most venerable shows dedicated to the pro-audio recording community is the Audio Engineering Society (AES) show that happens annually and alternates between New York and San Francisco—a great place to meet engineers, producers and manufacturers.

Below is a select list of trade shows and events. A comprehensive monthly calendar of global music trade shows and events can be found at Music Biz Events, found on the Internet at www.musicbizevents.com/mbize/events/.

Music Biz Events lists music conferences, gatherings, festivals, summits, and awards shows all over the world. It gives you an up-to-date description of each show, costs to attend, location and event contact information including a direct link to the event Website.

SXSW: South by Southwest (www.sxsw.com) is an annual tradeshow with 120 vendors and live band showcases every night. Over 2,000 bands play to industry executives, record labels, and music fans from around the world. Any band can submit its music to try to play at the show. For this March FestivalSXSW begins accepting artists submissions in August, with the deadline is early November.

ASCAP Expo: ASCAP's (www.ascap.com) music creator annual conference is dedicated to songwriting and composing. It helps you hear from industry panels, engage in writing and producing workshops, learn about new avenues for marketing and promoting your music, network with peers and music industry executives, and visit music trade exhibits.

The NAMM Show: Founded in 1901, NAMM (www.namm.org) has been driving the music products industry, enabling both large and small businesses to maximize productivity and reduce the costs of doing business. With more than 9,000 members in the United States and 100+ other countries, NAMM is ultimately dedicated to expanding the market and giving people of all ages the opportunity to experience the proven benefits of making music.

Popkomm: Popkomm (www.popkomm.de) is the international music and entertainment business trade show that takes place every October in Berlin, Germany. It was canceled for 2009 due to lack of attendance, but is slated to return in 2010 with a new format. Over 400 artists play in over 25 venues. Popkomm has a conference, which features over 850 exhibitors, along with feature speakers and panels from the leaders in the music industry. Popkomm accepts submissions on its Website to find bands to play at the festival.

North by Northeast: North by Northeast (www.nxne.com), Canada's music festival and conference, takes place every June in Toronto, Ontario. It features over 500 bands in 40 venues playing to 100,000 music fans and industry professionals. Conferences scheduled during the day feature conference panels and interviews with music industry professionals and companies.

WOMEX: WOMEX (www.womex.com) is the world's biggest professional music conference, trade fair and showcase for world, roots, folk, ethnic, traditional, alternative world, local and diaspora music.

The Great Escape Festival: This U.K. (www.escapegreat.com) festival features more than 200 bands in 25 venues over three days and occurs every May, featuring a music conference-style format with industry speakers, exhibitors and more.

Music Matters: The Asia Pacific music forum, Music Matters (www.musicmattersasia.com) takes place in June in Hong Kong with over 750 delegates including 78 speakers, 100 attending press, 80 sponsors and media partners, and 15 live acts performing at three separate music showcases.

New Music West: New Music West (www.newmusicwest. com) takes place every May in Vancouver, Canada. It features a conference and workshops for industry professionals and musicians. It features more than 250 bands playing to fans and industry professionals. NMW accepts submissions on its Website to find bands to play at the festival.

Dewey Beach Music Conference: The Dewey Beach Music Conference (www.deweybeachfest.com) takes place in Delaware every October for three nights. Artists and bands can attend workshops by industry professionals. Bands can submit their music to play.

Musikmesse: Musikmesse (www.musik.messefrankfurt.com) is the international fair for musical instruments, sheet music, music production, and music business connections. Musikmesse is held in Frankfurt, Germany. Here, you will find a complete range of products with everything required for making music, not to mention innumerable workshops, concerts, demonstrations and discussion events.

In the City: In the City (www.inthecity.co.uk) takes place every October in England and features industry professional panels and speakers and live music for three nights. In the City accepts submissions on its Website to find bands to play at the festival.

Metro Music Expo: Metro Music Expo (www.detroit. metromix .com) takes place in September in Novi, Michigan. This consumer expo/event has an extensive exhibit floor, panel discussions with industry insiders, clinics & demos on the newest equipment and live performances from some of the region's best talent. Musicians of all skill levels, music fans of all ages and those looking to launch a career in the music business will be able to test equipment, participate in panel discussions, explore gear clinics, browse rock photography exhibits, watch live music, shop for instruments and more.

Each of these events brings together different targeted communities of the industry. You will likely never be able to go to all of them, and some are even be restricted to industry professionals only so it's important that you pick and choose your events carefully. Be certain that they are relevant to your specific objectives. If you cultivate your local network carefully you will find opportunities to get invited to the industry-professionals-only gatherings as well. Membership with key organizations like The Recording Academy can pay off handsomely with member only benefits that can get you into both trade shows and events that would otherwise be closed to the general public. Think of it as an annual VIP pass to the local opportunity market.

Most conventions and trade shows will offer a list of registered attendees on the events Website and you should prepare your targeted "hit list" from this. At the convention there will most often be a published book listing all the registered attendees and their contact information—a goldmine of phone numbers and e-mail addresses. Here's where you can also find information about what products they represent and even what kind of music they are into. If possible, reach out to the people you think might present the most relevant opportunities in advance of the trade show. If at all possible, schedule a meeting well ahead of time, and then follow-up closer to the event.

COACH'S CORNER: Where do I Need to Be?

In order to effectively build a local network, you will have to evaluate the scene in your current city and determine if it's even possible where you live. There may be some good music in your town, but is there enough to support a production career? Penetrating the inner circles of the music industry will most often require that you relocate to an area that can support your objectives.

This is a big decision and one that requires some serious preparation and forethought. It's a shrinking one, but the world is still big—travel and see/ hear your community throughout the world while you're young enough to pull it off! Who knows where you'll settle down!

Make sure you are clear on your objectives before entering the event. Prepare yourself with the right materials that can help you get the job done and make sure to rehearse yourself so when the opportunity presents itself you don't stumble on your own words. Bring some business cards, promotional CDs, and résumés or one-sheets—make sure you have everything you need, and that it is organized and easy for you to access. Keep in mind that everyone is handing out stuff at these events, so forget about the over-bloated press kit. Just make sure that whatever you hand out looks professional and makes you stand out from the pack. That can be as simple as using brightly colored sleeves or creative and colorful graphics and artwork.

If you're trying to schedule a meeting with someone at one of these events, or if you're following up with them afterward, consider using professional phone etiquette for the call. Before you even pick up the phone to reach out to your desired contact, make sure you're prepared! Do some basic Web searches on the person you trying to reach to find their bio or any articles or Websites that describe who they are and what they do in the industry. I'm not talking about their shoe size or how many times they have been married or divorced—keep it professional.

COACH'S CORNER: Warming Up the Cold Call

Building your network serves multiple functions, including securing the all-important 'letter of referral' (or if possible an introductory phone call). I often receive cold calls from people I don't know, asking if I have five or ten minutes to spare and if I wouldn't mind them "picking my brain." I am generous with my time and love to offer advice, but the truth is, if I don't know you, I will be less inclined to invest much time (if any) in your cold call. This is not being callous—I need to be careful to manage my time efficiently. If I took every cold call that came into the office, it would jeopardize my own productivity. Now, on the other hand, if I receive a call from a colleague asking me if I wouldn't mind taking a few minutes to speak with a colleague of theirs, might this make a difference? Of course it would. Now, I am doing a favor for someone I know and trust which not only makes me feel good (I know I'm not wasting time) but it also puts their colleague in a position to actually get my time.

You should come from a place of awareness and respect about the person and their professional history—you'll be amazed at how far a little flattery might get you. Not overt, blatant flattery ("I'm your biggest fan!") but the kind that shows an understanding and appreciation for the hard work your contact has done to achieve their position in the industry. This is a great way to break the ice and opens the door for you to begin asking very targeted and pertinent questions that might very well open a door of opportunity for you. Besides, just about everyone likes to talk about themselves and everyone likes to hear positive feedback—or at least that they have a positive influence on someone out there!

Some of the top industry organizations (NARAS, NARIP, AES, etc.) are loaded with industry veterans and the most seasoned of veterans know how important it is to stay current and connected. That's exactly why you can be sure to find current and relevant professionals at all the trade shows and industry events. Whether they are speaking on a panel or helping organize the event, you can be sure that they too attend these shows and events to stay in the public's eye and network. The need for building and maintaining a strong network of industry associates never goes away. Staying current with up-to-date contacts is an art form. NARIP, for example, is dedicated to continuing education and networking for label executives and attorneys. While you may not qualify to join their ranks immediately, they are constantly producing educational events and networking mixers that can be attended for a relatively small entrance fee. These events can prove to be valuable in exposing yourself to new contacts as well as some very valuable—and current—information on industry trends.

When attending events like these, it's important that you be prepared—the other half of luck. Once you make the personal connection, follow it up with something to put in their hands with your contact info. Business cards are cheap and easy to make and are well worth the investment, even if they just have your name, e-mail and phone number. Since you are just getting your foot in the door, I suggest being creative with how you present yourself. If you are looking for work in a studio you might consider creating a card for yourself that says: "Studio Rat" or "Pro Tools Kid" or anything that might evoke a smile or momentary nod of appreciation.

COACH'S CORNER: Your Management "Assistant"

Having some good contact management software is invaluable, whether online, on your mobile or in a dedicated software app on your home computer. Contact software like ACT, NOW, Mac Address Book, Outlook or any of the many different ones available is a must! If you're budget-challenged (read: broke), there are numerous options available online. Google the phrase "free contact manager" and watch what comes up! All of these tools help you keep track of your ever-growing network as well setting valuable reminders for yourself on times and dates, like birthdays or follow-up calls. Nothing is worse than making a promise to call someone at a specific time and date and then forgetting to do it. This spells flake with a capital "F" and will guarantee that you never get another appointment or call back.

There are also many great mobile phone apps out there that can really help keep you organized and on your toes. A few of my favorite include: Omnifocus (great for keeping your to do's in order) and Evernote (great for keeping all your random notes, receipts and voice memo's organized and all in one place!). The best thing about them is how they will sync to your desktop and laptop so you're never without direction or purpose!

Again, keep it professional—don't be too cute or unseemly ("I'm a future rock star" can seem egotistical and can easily turn someone off). Cute cards can serve as conversational icebreakers and offer an immediate possibility of discussing your key objectives. They also serve as something to write on when getting someone else's contact information, so consider designing them with lots of blank space. You can always ask for their card too. If they don't have one, you can quickly jot down their info on one of your cards with a key phrase that will help you remember what it was you were talking about with them. During the course of a trade show or event, you can meet a lot of people, so having these notes to refer to afterwards can be invaluable.

After any show or event, it's important to spend some time evaluating the contacts you collected and entering them into your database. Cards and notes are great when you're on the move but at the end of the day, you'll need an organized way to track them. After all, if someone was actually interested in you but you lost their contact info (or never bothered to follow up with them), you'd have missed out on an opportunity.

Like many things in life, building your network is a numbers game—every new industry contact you develop creates the possibility of expanding your network with theirs. This process is exponential and, if done correctly, can open doors that you never thought existed. Be careful of becoming a network whore—having 2,500 contacts is useless if you have no relationship to them! Start with a set number in mind, like 20 to 30 individual contacts relative to your career objective. This will be the beginning of your roadmap into the industry. Often these contacts may not have the specific opportunity that you are looking for, but they may possibly know someone else in the industry that does. This is where your well-timed request for an introductory phone call or e-mail can make all the difference. In addition, many of these contacts are likely to be involved in social networking groups ("Pro Tools User Group" or "Record Label Executive Group" etc.), which are great resources for job opportunities, relationships and contact gathering.

Remember that the worst that can happen is they just say no. Get comfortable hearing 'no' (you'll hear it a lot in this business!) and learn to be gracious about it. Then go ask someone else! If you don't ask, you'll never find out what was possible. This process requires that you be thoughtful and considerate in your approach and never forget that a little humor and creativity can often go a long way. I can't repeat it enough: At the end of the day, this is a "people business" and people like to do business with people who are respectful, appropriate and whosec ompany they enjoy.

3

Change Is the Constant

"Forward, Never Straight"

DVD: Studio-Side Chat
Chapter 2: Music as Digital Media
Effect on major labels-leveling the
playing field: 7:27–9:30
DVD-ROM Support Doc:
"32 Different Ways Artists Can
Make Money"

There was a time when the music industry was made up of specialists—the songwriters wrote songs, the performers performed, engineers and producers recorded and produced and labels were run by businessmen. Needless to say, times have changed dramatically. The evolution of technology has lowered the barriers of entry (price, technical knowledge etc.) and allowed many more would-be artists to try their hand at producing and selling music. This change in technology and production process has opened the gates for a whole new era of recording artist/ entrepreneur (The "*entre-producer*"), but in turn has created a whole new breed of professional faced with the challenge of integrating many of the jobs that were once the role of seasoned veterans and specialists.

At the turn of the century, the Internet as a means of promoting and distributing music hit the industry hard. Many have referred to this as a "leveling of the playing field" between independent and major label artists and it's forever changed the way in which recording artists and labels operate.

"Artists are at a point where they realize going back to the old model doesn't make any sense. There is a hunger for a new way of doing things."—Brian Message, Manager, Radiohead. *New York Times*, July, 2009.

This, coming from the manager of a band who gave away its 2008 release "In Rainbows" for free (or whatever anyone would pay for it) in its pre-physical release digital download format.

Many brand-name artists seized this opportunity for change to break ties with the once-hallowed major labels that helped bring them to dominance. Granted, with name brands like The Beastie Boys and Nine Inch Nails, it's a lot easier to sell your own music. Independent artists just coming on to the scene lack the advantage of having an established brand.

However, industry veterans like Brian Message (and his company Polyphonic) are banking on the passion and entrepreneurial spirit of independent artists to make a go of financing and treating them just like any other startup business enterprise. Many artists have made successful careers out of the DIY approach. The fact is that we have now reached a time where this is no longer the alternative route but the norm. I'm not talking million dollar mansions and limousines—I'm talking about getting the opportunity to make a decent living doing what you love.

Navigating the Waters of Independence:

DVD: Studio-Side Chat
Chapter 2: Music as Digital Media

Creating something where there is nothing is no easy feat. This is the beating heart that drives the creative impulse of all would-be recording artists and musicians: to create through sound, music and image a connection with the public. When the connection is made, it brings with it the promise of an enduring career in the entertainment industry, but to endure means to never relent. This can be very challenging if your momentum and destiny are not in your control—something prevalent with many major labels.

The major labels are awash in artists that were signed but who's work never saw the light of day. They are seen as collateral damage of an industry that hedges its bets. The industry is filled with stories of hungry young artists being taken advantage of early in their careers: artists who signed away their publishing rights and even the rights to their name. For example, When artists signed a traditional major label deal in the '90s, they were generally given an advance equal to the amount a label felt comfortable they could profit from, ranging from $125,000 to $350,000.

Lets look at some of the ways this might not actually be a good deal, even though the advance money looks very appealing.

In order to recoup that investment and turn a profit on advances like these, the majors created artist deals that virtually guaranteed the artist would remain in debt to the label. Consider this example:

☞ An advance of $250,000 is given to the artist to create a record.

☞ The standard major label record deal is for 12 to 15 points. A twelve-point royalty actually means the artist is entitled to make 12% of the retail sales price of each full-length CD, minus some "standard" deductions, after recouping. "Recouping" means paying back all of the expenses from the artist's royalty (basically, running the label), in this case 12%. So, for example, if a CD sells for $14.99, a 12-point royalty would mean the artist was entitled to $1.80 per CD!

☞ The label then adds additional reductions including packaging defects and other ancillary and in many cases irrelevant costs, so then that $1.80 per CD gets whittled down to about $1.00 a CD.

☞ If an artist sells 200,000 CDs, then that $1.00-per-CD royalty is used to recoup the monies advanced to the band to create the recordings as well as any other money advanced for promoting, producing videos, and touring. So the $200,000 (200,000 CDs×$1.00/CD) goes to repaying the expenses, making it very difficult for the artists to actually earn any artists royalties beyond the original advance.

☞ In order to sell that quantity in today's economy it will cost between $250,000 and $1,000,0000 in marketing costs alone!

So you can see how rare it is for an artist to recoup. In fact, the artist's account is almost always in the negative, meaning more money was spent on the project than the artist was able to pay back from his or her $1.00-per-sold-CD as the rest of the money gets split between the label, the distributor and the retailer. The key to financial freedom for an artist signing a traditional major label deal is to secure as much money upfront as possible, and then to deliver the album for as little as possible and keep the overages. This was far easier to do in the '90s but now, with shrinking advances and labels looking to take control of every aspect of an artists' career, this has become far less desirable. There's a reason Prince carved the word "slave" into his beard even after having been advanced millions of dollars by Warner Bros. Records!

The current change in the music industry has opened the door for artists to build and craft their own careers by controlling both the ownership of their master recordings, publishing interests and all other revenue streams generated by touring, merchandising, licensing and product endorsements. Due in large part to the Internet and its ability to level the marketing side of the playing field, artists are now more willing to strike out on their own (or in tandem with an indie label who is more willing to create a true partnership with the artist). With fewer deals and smaller advances available with major labels than ever before, most artists are left with little choice.

The good news, and the hidden potential in all of this is that artists who succeed in navigating these waters can maintain ownership of all their master recordings and associated publishing and will be able to build a lasting career that puts them squarely in the drivers seat!

If an artist can manage this process effectively and come out with a professional and unique product, then their major challenge becomes the marketing and creation of an established brand in the eyes of the buying public. This is where the major labels still have dominance. The major labels are able to get major placements for their artists: touring, retail, endorsements, radio, video play, appearances on major awards shows, talk shows, and major publications etc. Indie labels have a harder time doing this with the same level of impact due to budgets. Also, major distribution takes precedent at retail stores over Indie distribution, making it easier to get CDs into stores through a major label.

More good news? New cost-effective channels have and continue to become regularly available for artists to promote themselves and get their music heard and bought. These new channels and the promise of true partnership between artists and their labels are the foundation of an industry being re-born. Together they offer the promise and hidden potential of many more lasting careers and job opportunities than would never ever have been afforded the light of day in an industry dominated by major labels.

Facts and Figures in the Music Business

"In order to change, one must believe that change is not only desirable, but possible. You must be the change you wish to see in the world . . ."—Mhatma Ghandi

**DVD: Studio-Side Chat
Chapter 1: The New Face of
the Music Business**
Independent artist
opportunity: 3:53–4:31

I have heard many veterans of the music industry say that illegal file sharing and digital cloning of CDs signaled the death of music sales. It is easy to forget that it wasn't so long ago that the major labels were claiming the demise of recorded music sales with the introduction of the cassette tape! Clearly one cannot dispute the fact that traditional music sales have seen a steep decline since the mid-1990s. The total revenues for CDs, vinyl, cassettes and digital downloads combined in the U.S. dropped from a high of $14.6 billion in 1999 to $10.4 billion in 2008. This downward trend is expected to continue for the foreseeable future.

Forrester Research—a technology and trend research company in Massachusetts—predicts that by 2013, revenues will reach as low as $9.2 billion. This dramatic decline in revenue has caused large-scale layoffs inside the industry, driven music retailers out of business (such as Tower Records in 2006) and forced record companies, record producers, studios, recording engineers and musicians to seek new business models. With many of the country's leading music-only stores now closed or out of business (Tower, Virgin, etc . . .), the leading physical music retailers are now major retail outlets like Walmart and Best Buy.

The IFPI (International Federation of the Phonographic Industry—www.ifpi.org) is a great resource for understanding the trends and numbers for global music sales. **Figure 3 A/B** shows the numbers posted by the IFPI for 2008 ("3A") and the trends being represented by the shifts between 2007 and 2008 ("3B").

A	Physical	Digital	Performance Rights	Total
USA	3,138.70	1,783.30	54.8	4,976.80
EUROPE	5,808.80	750.8	576.2	7,308.80
ASIA	3,600.90	1,063.60	108.1	4,772.70
LATIN AMERICA	430.30	62.6	25.7	518.60
GLOBAL	13,829.30	3,783.80	802.0	18,415.20

B	Physical	Digital	Performance Rights	Total
USA	-31.20%	16.50%	133.30%	-18.60%
EUROPE	-11.30%	36.10%	11.30%	-6.30%
ASIA	-4.90%	26.10%	14.60%	1.00%
LATIN AMERICA	-10.30%	46.60%	16.70%	-4.70%
GLOBAL	-15.40%	24.10%	16.20%	-8.30%

Figure 3 A/B: *2008 International Federation of the Phonographic Industry charts demonstrate a clear decline in CD sales and the rise in Internet sales of music. Figure 3A shows unit sales for 2008. Figure 3B illustrates the shift in trends between 2007 and 2008.*

Here are the definitions of these categories as stated by the IFPI:

☛ Physical sales refer to sales of physical units—CDs usually.

☛ Digital sales refer to sales via online (single track and album downloads, music video downloads, streams, bundles and kiosk sales) and mobile channels (master ringtones, single track downloads to mobile, ringback tones, music video downloads to mobile, streams, mono/polyphonic ringtone income, embedded music on mobile phones (preloaded), mobile bundles, greetings, and dedications income) and via subscriptions. Income from ad-supported services, mono/polyphonic ringtone income, and bundled subscriptions were included in the digital sales figures in 2008.

☛ Performance rights figures reflect monies received by record companies from collection societies for licenses granted to third parties for the use of sound recordings in music videos in broadcasting (radio and TV), public performance (nightclubs, bars, restaurants, hotels), and certain Internet uses.

COACH'S CORNER: The Big Players

Prior to December 1998 (according to the IFPI), the industry was dominated by what it referred to as the "big six major labels": Sony Music, BMG, Universal Music group, PolyGram, Warner Music and EMI. After the PolyGram-Universal merger, the 1998 market shares reflected a "Big Five", commanding 77.4% of the global market and independents making up 22.6% of the global market. According to an IFPI report published in August 2005, the "Big Four" (after Sony and BMG merged) accounted for 71.7% of retail music sales and independents accounted for 28.4%. Sales reports between the IFPI and the Nielsen Soundscan vary widely. Nielsen Soundscan shows independent music sales in 2005 to be at 18.13%!

Another organization like the IFPA and also at the center of the recording industry is the Recording Industry Association of America (RIAA), which tracks the buying trends for all forms of distributed music. Its members represent the major record companies that create, manufacture and/or distribute approximately 85% of all "legitimate" sound recordings produced and sold in the United States.

Based on 2008 RIAA research, sales of digital music as a whole continued growing at a rapid pace in 2008, and as of summer of 2009, constituted 32 percent of the total music sales market—valued at $2.7 billion in total shipments. "Digital music" is defined as including: single and album downloads, in-store kiosks, music video downloads, mobile (anything music-related purchased for your mobile phone/device), and subscriptions to streaming services. The sector with the largest growth is in digital downloads, which grew 30% to $1.6 billion!

This staggering growth figure clearly demonstrates the continued adoption of the digital music download model. It seems that music fans are increasingly comfortable buying full-length albums online, with digital album growth rates exceeding those of digital singles. On a dollar basis, digital albums grew from 25 percent of the download market in 2004 to 36 percent in 2008.

According to Nielsen, another industry sales-tracking company, physical album sales fell 20%, to 362.6 million units in 2008. Concurrently, sales of individual tracks rose 27%, to 1.07 billion, which financially failed to compensate for the drop in album sales. When this is added to both CDs and digital albums, the overall album unit decline in 2008 was 14% (635 million to 545 million). That's still bad news.

The RIAA states that distributions for digital performance rights, which include payments to artists and labels for web casting, satellite radio, and other digital music services, increased 74% to $82 million in 2008. Though currently a small component of the overall market, performance revenues represent an increasingly important piece of the music industry landscape as fans shift listening habits to digital formats.

Interestingly enough though, vinyl continued to stage a comeback in 2008, as the format more than doubled year-over-year to $57 million, the highest level since 1990. The rollout of vinyl—as both new releases and catalog material—was bolstered by audiophiles, DJs and devout fans. **Figure 4** (on page 54) shows these statistics more definitively.

There is other proof of the market's shift to independence. As of summer 2009, there were estimated to be over eight million music pages on the popular (Fox Interactive Media-owned) MySpace.com. One must be careful however to delineate carefully the difference between big budget, big artist promotion and My Space, self-funded, self promoted artists as the two are clearly *not* on the same playing field. This difference is where the majors still really matter and make a difference to the sales of a record—they can simply outspend anyone and get more attention. This gets more sales. Simple.

As lower-cost digital recording solutions continue to flood the market, it has created (and continues to create) a whole new breed of "bedroom" producers. Based on Nielsen's Soundscan reports (the independent tracker of music sales), more than 44,000 albums were released in the U.S. alone in 2008! Prior to 2008 annual averages of albums released in the U.S. ranged from 27,000 to 35,000. According to the RIAA, the major labels release about 7,000 new albums per year and less than 10% of them are profitable. These 7,000 albums account for more than 800 million CD units being shipped to stores. This is before we account for the 44,000 independent releases!

Manufacturers' Unit Shipments and Retail Dollar Value
(In Millions net after returns)

2008 Year-End Shipment Statistics

Digital

(Units shipped / dollar value)	1998	1999	2000	2001	2002	2003	2004	2005	2006	2007	% Change 2006-2007	2008	% Change 2007-2008
Download Single (units)							139.4	366.9	586.4	809.9	38.1%	1,033.0	27.5%
Download Single (value)							138.0	363.3	580.6	801.6	38.1%	1,022.7	27.6%
Download Album (units)							4.6	13.6	27.6	42.5	54.0%	56.9	33.9%
Download Album (value)							45.5	135.7	275.9	424.9	54.0%	568.9	33.9%
Kiosk (units)								0.7	1.4	1.8	28.5%	1.6	-8.7%
Kiosk (value)								1.0	1.9	2.6	38.1%	2.6	-1.2%
Music Video (units)								1.9	9.9	14.2	43.0%	20.8	46.7%
Music Video (value)								3.7	19.7	28.2	43.0%	41.3	46.7%
Mobile (units)							143.9	383.1	625.3	868.4	38.9%	1,112.3	28.1%
Mobile (value)							183.4	503.6	878.0	1257.2	43.2%	1635.4	30.1%
Subscription (units)								170.0	315.0	362.0	14.9%	338.4	-6.5%
Subscription (value)								421.6	773.8	880.8	13.8%	816.3	-7.3%
(units)								1.3	1.3	1.8	42.8%	1.6	-15.0%
(value)								149.2	206.2	201.3	-2.4%	188.2	-6.5%
Digital Performance Royalties							6.9	27.4	31.5	47.0	49.2%	81.8	74.1%

Physical

	1998	1999	2000	2001	2002	2003	2004	2005	2006	2007	% Change 2006-2007	2008	% Change 2007-2008
CD (units)	847.0	938.9	942.5	881.9	803.3	746.0	767.0	705.4	619.7	511.1	-17.5%	384.7	-24.7%
CD (value)	11,415.0	12,816.3	13,214.5	12,909.4	12,044.1	11,232.9	11,445.5	10,520.2	9,372.6	7,452.3	-20.5%	5,471.3	-26.6%
CD Single (units)	56.0	55.9	34.2	17.3	4.5	8.3	3.1	2.8	1.7	2.6	51.5%	0.7	-71.7%
CD Single (value)	213.2	222.4	142.7	79.4	19.6	36.0	14.9	10.9	7.7	12.2	59.0%	3.5	-71.3%
Cassette (units)	158.5	123.6	76.0	45.0	31.1	17.2	5.2	2.5	0.7	0.4	-41.2%	0.1	-62.8%
Cassette (value)	1,419.9	1,061.6	626.0	363.4	209.8	108.1	23.7	13.1	3.7	3.0	-18.4%	0.9	-70.7%
LP/EP (units)	3.4	2.9	2.2	2.3	1.7	1.5	1.4	1.0	0.9	1.3	36.6%	2.9	124.1%
LP/EP (value)	34.0	31.8	27.7	27.4	20.5	21.7	19.3	14.2	15.7	22.9	46.2%	56.7	147.7%
Vinyl Single (units)	5.4	5.3	4.8	5.5	4.4	3.8	3.8	2.3	1.5	0.6	-58.5%	0.4	-30.9%
Vinyl Single (value)	25.7	27.9	26.3	31.4	24.9	21.5	21.5	13.2	9.9	4.0	-59.6%	2.9	-27.4%
Music Video (units)	27.2	19.8	18.2	17.7	14.7	19.9	19.9	33.8	23.2	27.5	18.6%	12.8	-53.6%
Music Video (value)	508.0	376.7	281.9	329.2	288.4	399.9	607.2	602.2	451.1	484.9	7.5%	218.9	-54.9%
DVD Video (units)	0.5	2.5	3.3	7.9	10.7	17.5	29.0	27.8	22.3	26.6	19.4%	12.3	-53.8%
DVD Video (value)	12.2	66.3	80.3	190.7	236.3	369.6	551.0	539.8	442.8	476.1	7.5%	215.7	-54.7%
Total Units	1123.9	1160.6	1079.2	968.5	859.7	798.4	814.1	748.7	548.2	543.9	-16.1%	401.8	-26.1%
Total Value	13,711.2	14,584.7	14,323.7	13,740.9	12,614.2	11,854.4	12,154.7	11,195.0	9,868.6	7,985.8	-19.1%	5,758.5	-27.9%
Total Retail Units	1,123.9	869.7	788.6	733.1	675.7	658.2	687.0	634.8	558.8	464.4	-16.1%	348.7	-24.9%
Total Retail Value	13,711.2	13,048.0	12,705.0	12,388.8	11,549.0	11,053.4	11,423.0	10,477.5	9,269.7	7,495.3	-19.1%	5,474.3	-27.9%

Total Digital & Physical

	1998	1999	2000	2001	2002	2003	2004	2005	2006	2007	% Change 2006-2007	2008	% Change 2007-2008
Total Units	1,123.9	1,060.6	1,079.2	968.5	859.7	798.4	958.0	1,301.8	1,588.5	1,774.3	11.7%	1,852.5	4.4%
Total Value	13,711.2	14,584.7	14,323.7	13,740.9	12,614.2	11,854.4	12,345.0	12,296.9	11,758.2	10,372.1	-11.8%	8,480.2	-18.2%

% of Shipments	2005	2006	2007	2008
Physical	91%	84%	77%	68%
Digital	9%	16%	23%	32%

Retail value is value of shipments at recommended or estimated price

[1] Includes Singles and Albums
[2] Includes Master Ringtones, Ringbacks, Music Videos, Full Length Downloads, and Other mobile
[3] Weighted Annual Average
[4] Estimated payments in dollars to artists and record companies distributed by SoundExchange. Amounts based on prior year's collections and airplay
[5] While broken out for this chart, DVD Video Product is included in the Music Video totals
[6] Total includes Cassette Single, DVD Audio and SACD shipments not broken out separately in this report
[7] Units total includes both album and singles, and does not include subscriptions or royalties

Permission to cite or copy these is hereby granted, as long as proper attribution to the Recording Industry Association of America

Figure 4: *RIAA sales charts for the fiscal year ending 2007.*

New Media

The entertainment industry as a whole lives and dies by the adoption rate of new technology—most of these technologies come with pros and cons. In the end however, their future is determined by whether or not the buying public is willing to play along and back it with their entertainment dollars. In the music industry there have been numerous excellent examples of this—ever wonder what happened to the 8-track or cassette?

Come and Get it!

DVD: Studio-Side Chat
"Media and Quality"
Other media formats and the resurgence of vinyl: 25:38–27:40

When the cassette tape came into prominence, the music industry as a whole was very concerned that the ability to easily record material would result in a large black market for pirated music that would eat away at their profits (sound familiar?). Of course cassette copies were subject to quality degradation and this helped to ease their fears. After all, cassettes don't sound as good as records ... right?

As a great example of finding the "hidden potential" in cassettes, the industry began to see the benefits of this new technology as they were able to resell large amounts of their pre-existing catalogs to a whole new segment of music buyers. During the 1980s, the cassette's popularity grew greatly as a result of portable pocket recorders and hi-fi players such as Sony's Walkman and the large install base of cassette players in automobiles.

This process repeated itself againâ with the introduction of the Compact Disc, and this is where the story gets interesting. Initially the music industry presented the CD as a new, high-quality digital medium that was indestructible, ultimately cheaper to produce and would eventually lower the retail cost of music. The major labels and their technology counterparts realized they had much to gain financially from this new format, as the buying public would replace their vinyl and cassettes—again—with CDs—if the quality was considered to be good enough.

This was a major win for the established industry as they began to realize huge profits from releasing both new and old catalogs on the new format. The first major artist to have his entire catalog converted to CD was David Bowie, whose 15 studio albums were made available by RCA in February 1985, along with four Greatest Hits albums (according to the *New Schwann Record & Tape Guide*, Volume 37, No. 2, Feb. 1985). In

1988, 400 million CDs were manufactured by 50 pressing plants around the world but they never fulfilled their promise of lower prices, despite the lower manufacturing costs (noted Glenn Baddeley in *Mac Audio News,* No. 178, Nov. 1989).

As CD sales began to peak in the mid-1990s, so too came a new media technology that would both catch the music industry by surprise and forever change the playing field. It's of note that numerous different formats of CDs were created in an attempt to sell these catalogs to the public yet again. These included the enhanced CD, CD Video, CD-ROM, CD-Text, the laserdisc, the MiniDisc, the 5.1 Music Disc, the Super Audio CD (SACD) and others. It turns out that the public wasn't interested in multiple formats but in higher quality or increased convenience only.

The MP3 is a patented digital audio encoding format that uses a lossy data compression scheme (data was purposefully left out, but the perceived quality was close to the original) and many would argue that its introduction radically altered the habits of the music-buying public. The idea behind this lossy format was to greatly reduce the file size of digital music without too much noticeable degradation of the sound quality. A standard Red Book audio file (CD quality) takes up ten megabytes (10 megs) of hard disc space per stereo minute while a 128 Kbps (kilobytes per second) MP3 file takes up approximately one tenth of the size (1 meg). This encoding scheme is very practical for storing and creating large catalogs of digital MP3 music libraries as well as being able to post and share them via the Internet.

From the first half of 1994 through the late 1990s, MP3 files began to spread on the Internet. The popularity of MP3s began to rise rapidly with the advent of Nullsoft's audio player Winamp (released in 1997), and the Unix audio player mp123, which both allowed the files to be easily played on a PC. This lead to the creation of peer to peer file sharing networks. In November 1997, the Website www.mp3.com was offering thousands of MP3s created by independent artists for free!

The small size of MP3 files enabled widespread peer-to-peer (P2P) file sharing of music ripped from CDs. The site supporting this was Napster, launched in 1999. To this day, there are many options for sharing files on the Internet including Gnutella, Kazaa, Limewire, and BitTorrent. With these networks, both users and the network of users they access are completely anonymous—a program downloaded to the users computers allows them to connect to the network. The user can then search the shared media on other users' computers and download this media from them across the Internet. These networks allow the sharing of any type of digital content, including songs, DVD-quality movies, computer programs and video games.

The ease of creating and sharing MP3s resulted in widespread copyright infringement. Digital files were distributed to network users that were not authorized to own them by either the artists or their labels—users never paid for them. While the MP3 and its ease of download made file sharing easy and convenient, and energized the public about music in general, it clearly did not boost sales. Major record companies argued that this free sharing of music reduced sales, and called it "music piracy."

The most surprising result of MP3s has been the public's blatant lack of concern for the artists, the labels and the quality of the music in general (remember that MP3 is a lossy compression and not nearly as high-quality as CDs). As new technology was being developed to increase the quality of recordings, the mass consuming public had set off on a feeding frenzy of zero-cost, lower-quality MP3s. The decline of CD sales continues to be blamed on Internet piracy and illegal downloading. In 2004, the Justice Department of the Federal Government even created special task forces to increase criminal prosecution of copyright infringers.

Oh, No You Don't! (DRM)

Labels had become victims of their own "re-sell the catalog in a new format" game and the buying public was fully prepared to show no mercy. The major labels along with the RIAA began combating the piracy of the Internet with a barrage of lawsuits against companies like Napster as well as individuals accused of large scale file sharing. They also instituted a new format of CD encrypted with Digital Rights Management (DRM) schemes that would prevent the unsuspecting public from extracting the music on CDs and converting them to MP3 files. These CDs were not actually Red Book audio CDs at all and were actually a form of CD-ROM that consumers could no longer play on their computers and many of which could not even play in many standard CD players! Sony BMG introduced new DRM technology that installed DRM software on users' computers without clearly notifying the user or requiring consent.

Among other things, the DRM CDs, when inserted into a computer, would install software that created a severe security vulnerability others could exploit (read: it opened your computer to malware and viruses). When the nature of the DRM involved was made public much later, Sony initially minimized the significance of the vulnerabilities its software had created, but was eventually compelled to recall millions of CDs, and released several attempts to patch the surreptitiously included software.

Several class action lawsuits were filed, which were ultimately settled by agreements to provide affected consumers with a cash payout or album downloads free of DRM (according to Robert McMillan's "Article Settlement Ends Sony Rootkit Case", in *PC World*, May 23, 2006). The result was a wave of negative press, which ultimately forced them to stop publishing DRM CDs.

In May of 1998, Congress passed the Digital Millennium Copyright Act in an effort to protect the labels and artists and the DRM technology's being used to protect their intellectual property from piracy. Most people argue that this ultimately did little to stave off piracy—once file sharing had entered the world of personal computing the proverbial cat had been let out of the bag and nothing was going to get it back in again.

Like with all great demises, there are always those visionaries who are able to see great opportunity (aka, hidden potential) where others see nothing but doom and gloom. One such visionary was Steve Jobs, CEO and founder of the personal computer company Apple, now the largest retail seller of digital music files on the Internet. After many "back room" meetings and much negotiation, Mr. Jobs was the first to be able to convince the major labels that they had no choice but to embrace the new digital medium. He presented a new way for the majors to capitalize on the MP3 revolution by allowing them to legitimately sell their catalogs of music on the Internet via his new platform, iTunes.

In order to do so, he argued that he could imbed a form of DRM into the files that would prevent buyers of these files from excessive file sharing. He was able to use this as the bait to lure in the majors. However, the DRM imbedded in the music originally sold on iTunes only allowed the music to be played through iTunes and the portable devices made by Apple, the iPod. This clever tactic allowed Apple to gain an early competitive edge on the digital music marketplace.

As competitors quickly saw the massive potential in this, they too attempted to follow suit. This gave rise to many other digital retailers of music on the Internet, many of whom started by selling independent music not in the control of the majors.

However, they all quickly realized that—without the major label catalogs—they would be relegated to selling much less volume than Apple was capable of. Once the major labels began to realize what they had done they also knew that they could not allow the virtual monopoly granted to Apple and that they had to level the playing field and allow their music to be digitally sold by others as well.

As this new sales channel was taking hold with the public, many new players entered the market including: Walmart, Amazon, Rhapsody, Beatport, Pandora and others, all vying for position in this uncharted and unregulated marketplace. This gave rise to a new breed of digital distributor—an aggregator of music to all the new retail portals. Not unlike the distributors of records and CDs, this aggregator would negotiate deals with the labels to distribute their music to as many outlets as possible. This was necessary to minimize confusion and create a standard by which files would be formatted and delivered for sale with the necessary metadata and artwork. The metadata was critical information regarding the music and its makers and the copyright information all embedded into the digital file.

This data would be used to categorize and organize a music library as well as facilitate new accounting systems by which both the labels and artists would be paid for their digital downloads. Numerous new players entered into the arena to tackle this daunting task including pioneers like IODA (The Independent Online Distribution Alliance) as well the online giant The Orchard, long-time independent music champion CD Baby and a small San Francisco-based company called InGrooves.

At the turn of the millennium, it became evident that Internet based sale and enjoyment of music was here to stay. Service providers like Pandora, Live365, and Rhapsody had given rise to a new model of Internet radio and the copyright owners and publishers were screaming for the need to track and monetize the copyrights and publishing revenue due them. Like radio, when a song is played, an artist should be paid. As this Internet listening system was unregulated at the time, no artists were being paid for these performances, which, in turn, gave rise to a new Performance Rights organization, SoundExchange. Its primary function is to track, collect and pay royalties to artists whose music is streamed or performed via the Internet and satellite radio. (Organizations like BMI, ASCAP, and SESAC collect royalties for writers and publishers whose music is played on terrestrial radio, film and cable TV.)

In 2000, SoundExchange set out to lobby congress for new laws entitling copyright owners and artists to collect performance royalties where there had previously been none. The Digital Performance in Sound Recordings Act of 1995 and the Digital Millennium Copyright Act of 1998 together granted a performance right for sound recordings publically performed via certain kinds of digital transmissions, but it was not until the creation of SoundExchange that there came to be a specific entity to advocate, account and collect for the artists and writers whose intellectual property (the songs and their recordings) was being played (streamed) via the Internet.

Initially, much controversy surrounded SoundExchange as it was an unincorporated division of the RIAA. In 2003 it was spun off as an independent and non-profit organization, but many to this day still point to its unwillingness to support the Internet Radio Equality Act because of its origin as an arm of the major labels whose publishing interests it seeks to protect. Many webcasters feared for the future of their existence as they were forced to pay higher royalties than satellite radio in addition to artist performance royalties that terrestrial radio had historically never had to pay. As of the writing of this text, many webcasters (including Pandora) have resolved their royalty feuds with Sound Exchange and are proving they can be profitable and pay the artists their fare share.

Central to the administration of publishing rights and also excellent resources for information and an understanding of how these rights work and earn money are the main three U.S. performance rights organizations: ASCAP, BMI and SESAC. All three respective Websites (www.bmi.com, www.ascap.com, and www.sesac.com) offer a plethora of legal and practical information about music publishing and allow you to become a registered writer and/or publisher. This allows them to track performances of your work and collect and distribute royalty payments to you! As previously mentioned, the other very important site to familiarize you with all the royalties based around web streaming and the lobbying for artists performance rights on terrestrial radio in the form of the Performing Rights Act, is SoundExchange (www.soundexchange.com).

Video Games—the New Frontier

Based on the decline in CD and music sales, one must ask: Where are the big growth opportunities and what are the buying trends of the public who drive them? If you look at those vying

DVD: Studio-Side Chat
"**Media and Quality**"
Licensing as a means
of increasing your
fan base 34:03–36: 34

for your entertainment dollar today compared to that of only fifteen years ago, you would see the enormous growth in both opportunity and competition. Where once the single and album formats dominated, now there are a plethora of choices for both purchasing and consuming music. These include the numerous online music retailers, like iTunes, Amazon, and Beatport, as well as the numerous streaming Web radio broadcasts like Pandora, Last.fm, Rdio and OurStage.

So too are the numerous other ways to entertain yourself including: the 500 channels on your cable service, the millions of videos on YouTube (not to mention millions of Websites and MySpace pages), the never-ending stream of Hollywood blockbuster movies, the thousands of independently produced films every year, both small and large artist/band tours and the numerous streaming music models. Of all these, what is the biggest grossing sector of the entertainment industry today? Video games.

Just like film and television, video games depend on strong musical sound tracks, dialog, and sound effects to make them compelling, realistic and exciting. This has proven to be a boon to those in the music and sound industry that have chosen to embrace and rise up to the challenges of producing audio for games. There was a time when audio for games meant nothing more than a series of blips and bleeps but now, video games developers are hiring sound designers, music editors, audio engineers, in house audio leads, music directors and world class composers to realize their sound tracks. Technology for gaming has accelerated at light speed as game boxes like the X-Box 360, Sony Playstation 3 and Nintendo Wii are now employing the highest quality audio and video playback systems available and the industry has even given rise to its own networking group: The Game Audio Network Guild (GANG).

Unlike sound for film and television, game audio requires a special set of skills beyond music production. Game audio doesn't work like CDs or films, which never change from viewing to viewing. Games never stop changing—every game play is different and the way the sound and music is played needs to adapt to the player (not the other way around), known as adaptive audio. In order to compose music or sound for adaptive playback, you'll need the standard skill of scoring music, but you'll also need to know how to score for non-linear and adaptive game play, as well as implementation tools that get the sound into the game.

DIAMOND IN THE ROUGH: GANG Activity

GANG (www.audiogang.org) is a non-profit organization that seeks to empower the game audio community by providing resources, education, and recognition for its members. Historically, a guild was a trade organization that monitored and controlled the licensing of a particular art or craft. In the renaissance, it functioned according to the old master and apprentice paradigm. GANG seeks to mimic this through its numerous membership types that include: Student, Apprentice, Associate and Professional. The Professional membership is divided into Bronze, Silver, Gold, Platinum and Diamond levels, the last of which requires 25 years professional experience and a host of other criteria. GANG awards are given annually at the Game Developers Conference (GDC) as a reward and acknowledgement of excellence and creativity in the field of game audio. Under the leadership of GANG president Paul Lipson (and Pyramind COO/ Composer!), GANG has (as of summer 2009) grown to over 2,500 members in over 30 countries!

So why exactly are video games such a big deal in the audio producing world?

As stated by Gamasutra.com, a leading video game industry web portal and according to a study from ABI Research (www .abiresearch.com), a market intelligence company specializing in global connectivity and emerging technology, the video game industry is expected to double in sales from 2005's $32.6 billion to $65.9 billion in 2011. The research firm indicates that the growth will take place as a result of online and mobile gaming becoming more popular.

To put this in perspective, we must realize that the global commercial film industry is approximately a $15-billion dollar industry (about half of gaming). As a point of comparison the total worldwide feature film revenue for major U.S. studios is expected to grow from $34.9 billion in 2007 to $41.6 billion by the end of 2011(Business Wire, 5.20.2008).

ABI Research predicts that the online game segment—which includes online-focused games for PC, consoles, and handheld systems—will grow by 95% annually until 2011, at which time it will likely be the dominating force in the market. Traditional single-player games are expected to remain high sellers, but will not see as much growth as their online counterparts.

Many had thought the massive video game industry to be recession-proof but the first half of 2009 proved that this was not necessarily the case. This theory is based on the premise that people tend to stay home during hard times, instead of spending money on big vacations and family outings. Add to that the large number of hours that gamers spend playing, and it's easy to assume that the long-term entertainment value of gaming works well in down economies.

However, according to the market research firm NPD Group Inc., sales of video games and their associated consoles in the United States fell 31% in June of 2009 to 1.2 billion, down from 1.7 billion in June of 2008. Of course, what is most telling is how games perform in the final quarter of any year—the critical holiday season when game publishers reap the bulk of their

COACH'S CORNER: Gaming Revenues Up—Way Up!

"The online console gaming market is set to take off, as the new generation of consoles arrives with advanced networking and online gaming capabilities, The ability to download game demos, buy casual as well as full-fledged console games, and access advanced content, including HD video, will result in "online" becoming the key technology component of gaming for this and subsequent console generations. Gaming has become a mass-market entertainment industry on a par with TV, movies and music, segments such as video game advertising, set to become a market worth close to $30 billion by 2011, will result in the further maturing of this industry. The ability to play music and media from powerful consoles and handhelds will drive overall industry growth as consumers begin to view gaming devices as one-stop-shop entertainment platforms."—Nich Maragos, in "Game Industry Revenue Expected To Double By 2011" new article on www.gamasutra.com, Feb 16th, 2006.

revenue. Regardless of the economic downturn of 2008 to 2009, the video game industry is indisputably a powerhouse in the entertainment industry.

So what does all this mean for those seeking a career in music or audio production?

With the significant installed user base of Sony's Playstation II and III, Microsoft's X-Box 360, and Nintendo's Wii and DS game boxes and with the impending tidal wave of online gaming, there is likely to be a continuously large appetite for new game titles by the public. This means significant employment opportunities for those with the right skill sets to help produce all these titles—the same group of game sound experts today can't fill the bill! New talent will be needed to ramp up game production and delivery to this hungry market.

In order to navigate the waters of employment in the video game industry, it is important to understand the game companies themselves and their production processes. Like all industries, there are many people and business segments that come together to bring a game to market. Of particular noteworthiness is the talent layer, made up of game developers, designers, and artists that work as either individual contractors or as part of a company. This asset creation and implementation is the area where employment opportunities abound for composers, sound designers, music editors, sound engineers and all sound creatives.

Often major game publishers like Electronic Arts (EA) or Sony will have their own in-house game development teams, many of which are actually their own companies! These giants of the industry can afford to outfit their own studios and maintain large staffs year round to support the production of their never-ending pipeline of games. Other smaller companies will staff up as needed during cycles of production then downsize when the games are done—or they'll partner up with the services division of their publishing partners.

Sony Computer Entertainment America (SCEA—makers of the PlayStations) and Microsoft Game Studios (MGS—makers of the Xbox) are both good examples of this as they seek to create incentives for developers to produce titles for their hardware. SCEA maintains significant audio production facilities and staff in the San Francisco Bay Area as well as Santa Monica and San Diego. Electronic Arts (EA) has significant studios also in the Bay Area as well as Vancouver, Canada. Microsoft has large recording and audio production facilities on its campus in Washington State and Lucasarts has significant facilities in the San Francisco Bay Area. These, of course are some of the biggest, but even the smallest of game developers require audio development for sound effects, music and dialog.

As the larger companies often house their own studios and talent, earning work with them is more difficult as positions do not frequently become available. Often the smaller developers present the best opportunities for finding contract-based audio work as they are more inclined to outsource their work as development ramps up. This is much more cost effective, as they can rely on the resources and talent of other facilities without having to maintain the large overhead required to maintain a year-round staff. A significant sector of this hire-as-needed game company is found in the casual games market—generally defined as games targeted at a mass audience that have simple rules with no extended time commitment or special skills by the player. They are usually played on a personal computer or online in web browsers.

As the music industry wrestles with piracy and royalty issues due to the MP3 file format and the Internet, the video game industry races ahead undaunted. Games are very difficult to pirate and as such, have maintained a solid profit margin. With projected growth set to explode (due to Internet based multiplayer titles and a loyal fan base hungry for new games), this new media format is here to stay. Of particular interest to the music industry is how the video game industry has been helping both new and established recording artists by licensing their music for use in games. Additionally, due to games that let the user feel like they are performing the music (as in Rock

COACH'S CORNER: The "Hidden" Gaming Market

Every month, an estimated 200 million consumers play casual games online, many of whom do not normally regard themselves as gamers, or fans of video games, according to "Casual Games Market Report 2007" in the 10/29/2007 Casual Games Association.

Band by Harmonix and Guitar Hero by Activision), video games have become both a sales and discovery tool for the emerging and legacy artist.

One champion of this movement to bridge the gaming and music worlds together is Steve Schnur, the Worldwide Executive for Music and Music Marketing at Electronic Arts. (FYI, EA is the largest video game producer in the world.) It is also home to some of the most famous game titles including: Madden NFL Football, The Sims, and Medal of Honor. Prior to joining the EA executive team for music Steve Schnur had a long history as a veteran record industry pro, working as an executive for numerous record labels including Arista, Elektra, Chrysalis, and Capitol Records. He has made it known in numerous interviews that his move into the gaming industry was done with the intention of creating synergies between the video game and music worlds. During his tenure at EA, Schnur has partnered with major and independent labels to create opportunities to feature new music to both enhance the gaming experience and to create channels through which gamers can purchase the music they have "discovered" in the game.

Another great example of games and music working together happened in July of 2009, when Harmonix announced a bold new move to capitalize on new music discovery and the ability to purchase music through gaming.

The announcement of the "Rock Band Network" on the Gamasutra Website stated:

"Rock Band users will soon be able to record and sell their own music tracks through the game's online store ... The move is reminiscent of developer Neversoft's song creation utility in Guitar Hero World Tour, but is considerably more ambitious. While the Guitar Hero solution was limited to synthesized and sampled music, Rock Band's allows users to record their own material from scratch using a version of the Reaper audio workstation as well as Harmonix's own Magma tool for PC."

This marked the beginning of what many hope will be a great opportunity for both emerging and established artists. Tony Kiewel, head of A&R for Sub Pop records is quoted in Billboard.biz as saying that his label was expecting to submit songs from its upcoming 2009 fall releases as well as bigger past releases. You can expect a huge swelling of bedroom producers to join the network as well! As of the end of 2008 the combined user install (total units sold) in the United States of the three major game consoles—The Nintendo Wii, Microsoft's X-Box 360, and the Sony Playstation 3—was over 30 million, according to James Brightman in *GameDaily*, November 14, 2008.

That means nearly one in every ten people in the United States owns at least one of these boxes! Currently the largest install base is the Wii, with over 13 million units, due mostly in part to its lower price point and broad appeal to children. The X-Box and the PS3 are by far the more sophisticated game boxes and are expected to ramp up in numbers as more titles and online features become available. The X-Box is currently second in installed systems with approximately 12 million and the PS3 at six million.

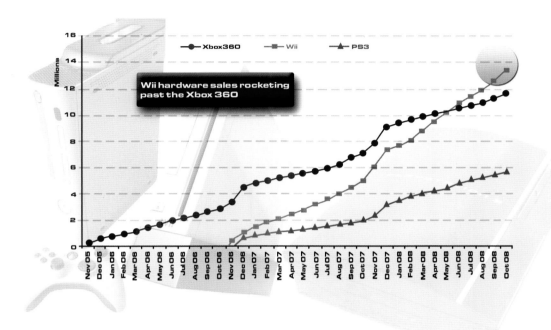

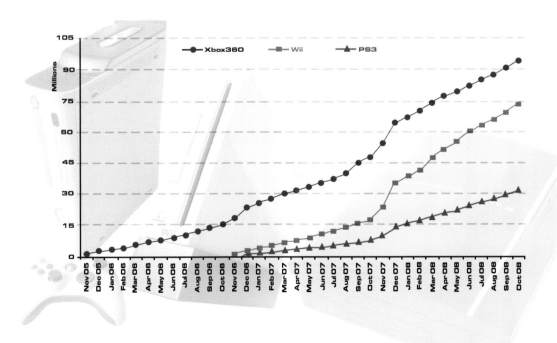

Figure 5A/B: *Sales reports of hardware console gaming units ("A") and software gaming units ("B").*

The Future's Up to You

As of this writing, the music industry finds itself wedged between the past and the future. The established ways of doing business have shifted, due to technological advances in production and distribution, from one where major labels own the musical rights and sales channels to one where the artist owns those rights. Developments in digital audio, computing, the Internet, and production equipment have given artists unprecedented access to the tools and power to create and market their own music, reaping the majority of the sales revenue!

While CD sales continue to slide, they are still a viable means of revenue generation with a vibrant (albeit shrinking) market. However, these shifts in technology present "hidden potentials"—opportunities for success—to those who can see where those potentials are. Just as the major labels sought to exploit the CD technology to boost sales by re-selling their music catalogs in the face of potential piracy, the MP3 technology and the Internet has given that potential back to the artist! The opportunities for success in the music business are ripe for the hungry, passionate and dedicated artists who can produce, market, and sell their own music without help.

Along with these shifts in technology, video games and computer games have presented an entirely new market for sales. The growth of this sector conitnues to dwarf the music and film industries combined and it too presents plenty of hidden potentials to people seeking to enter this industry. From sound designers, implementers, dialog recordists, editors, and composers who seek to become in-house game audio personnel to the artists who seek to place their music in these games, there is plenty of opportunity for those who seek it out!

I encourage you to follow through on your goals and dreams and suggest that you begin as I have my "Planning for Success" students start—by developing your Vision Statement and beginning to chart out your path through this business. Try to envision yourself in the perfect role and try to envision all of the efforts that might be required of you. Are you up to the task?

If so, get started—now.

Don't forget to keep your eyes peeled for that next opportunity and be sure to be prepared for it. Do your homework—develop your social network, get your résumé package together (the next section of this text), begin to lay out the business you want to start or at least, the employers you'd like to approach. Remember that being lucky is better than being good!

Most of all, stay true to your dreams—even if the road to them winds ever forward, and never straight . . .—*Gregory J. Gordon*

Introduction: Meet Tess Taylor

As you saw in Gregory J. Gordon's writing in the last section, there are many organizations in support of our industry that can help you further your career by growing your professional network. One of those organizations is NARIP—the National Association of Recording Industry Professionals. Tess Taylor is the founder and CEO of NARIP (www.narip.com).

Tess makes her living organizing and running seminars in markets all across the country related to the music business—from résumé writing to mock record deal negotiations. She's an absolute authority on the subject of the music business and how to get in—and stay in—the business.

Her take on résumé writing is unique and absolutely valid—in this business or any other. She's seen it all and knows what works and what doesn't. While Greg has laid out the landscape of how the music business really works (remember the hidden potential?), Tess offers specific actions to take when starting to break into the business.

If you're trying to work in the music business and are apply-ing for jobs, stop. Read Tess's writing first and take a look at your résumé. Is yours the winning one? Are you sure? Odds are, it needs a tune-up and Tess is just the coach for the job!

Even though I co-own my own company, and am in no danger of changing jobs, her writing inspired me to re-tool my résumé. You should follow suit.

Right now.

—Matt Donner

CHAPTER 5

Got Hustle?

These days, the career terrain—whether for audio professionals or enrolled or freshly graduated students—resembles the Chinese curse, "May your life be interesting!" Very interesting indeed!

The common denominator of those who succeed in our industry is not talent, it's perseverance and hustle! In the music business, hustle is as important as talent if not more so.

"Everyone has talent. What is rare is the courage to follow the talent to the dark place where it leads".—Erica Jong, novelist and poet

A degree and skills are not enough to get a gig. Advertised jobs as a producer, engineer, mixer, sound designer or audio professional are not abundant. In fact, they're practically non-existent. But it doesn't mean that these gigs don't exist.

"What element of the grateful world will receive me and give me a great job?" is an attitude typical among many students and recent graduates, and not just in audio engineering.

You've got to leave that notion behind, get over your shyness and get busy. Hustle means finding the unpublicized jobs or creating your own. It means having the confidence to introduce yourself to new people, ask questions, to insert yourself (politely) into situations and to create from scratch a gig that suits you. Hustle means coming to the table (or the studio) with the confidence of a bullfighter that you can and will contribute to the project at hand, and make no excuses.

The Bad News
. . . .

Many large and legendary recording studios have closed as they were unable to keep their doors open with the evaporation of large recording budgets, which were once standard. Major labels are no longer willing (or able) to write many large checks for production and studio work, plus high-end low-cost recording technology makes it easy for everyone to get into the audio production game. This floods the marketplace with competition, even if many of these newbies aren't as skilled and persistent as you.

People flock to music and entertainment hubs like Los Angeles, New York and Nashville from across the country and around the world. Singers, musicians, composers, marketers, publicists, lawyers, artist managers, producers, audio engineers, sound designers, mixers and professionals of every shape and size arrive every day by the truckload in these entertainment capitals. Talented people from around the world contribute to projects via the Internet and high-speed connections. Pro audio schools are enrolling and graduating record numbers of students.

The competition is daunting.

The Good News
. . . .

Even so, it's more important to focus on the opportunity that is more abundant than ever for those who know where and how to look. Talent with perseverance will always find a way. The industry is changing quickly—bold and talented people are in a position to create new models and paths for themselves, and influence the destiny of music and artistry in ways that weren't possible before. These are exciting times!

You can and will get what you want if you focus, create clear goals on paper and in your mind, and get in the game with the right tools and attitude.

I have helped hundreds of people get jobs and have connected people to thousands of opportunities through the organization I run—the National Association of Record

Industry Professionals (NARIP). I understand what buyers (employers) want and need, and I hire people, too. My advice comes from experience, but if you discover a better way to do anything I suggest here, then do it! And please let me know about it, too! Nothing is written on stone tablets, which is Success Tip #1.

You'll find strategies here about how to write a résumé, put yourself in the path of opportunity and create it for yourself, plus key skills and attitudes that will set you apart.

These have all worked for me, and they will for you, too.

Before You Create Your Résumé (or . . . "How to Market Your Most Important Product—You!")

Whether you're an audio engineering student, a recent grad looking for your first job or a professional with decades of production and audio experience, advancing your career in today's competitive entertainment industry depends upon on skills, research, and preparation—and connections. To connect is to be human, and the best way to connect is to treat others as you would like to be treated. Sound familiar? It's the Golden Rule, the best rule of all.

Most people do not get jobs through blind mailing of their résumés to employers whom they don't know, no matter how skilled. They get their jobs because they know somebody, or somebody knows them. The U.S. Department of Labor released statistics that 80 to 90 percent of people looking for jobs locate them through referrals or networking. This hasn't changed. Most business is done this way, through referrals of people you know and people who know you. Your network is everything. And your network is probably better than you think. Establishing contact first (either casually, through volunteering, mutual friends and co-workers, fellow students and teachers) and following up with your résumé will put you more than a step ahead, especially if you do this consistently.

Preparing a résumé that "sells" you to an employer is an important tool in your job search. While it's critical that your résumé be a highly polished, succinct and ruthlessly edited document (which you should continue to update and refine throughout your career) it is generally not what will get you in the door—your network will.

Mass mailing won't get you through, but personalization and human-to-human contact does. One of the easiest and most effective ways to get in touch is with the power of the personal handwritten note, and this goes beyond résumés and interview follow-ups. Can you remember the last time you received a handwritten note in the mail? When stacked against all of the bills and mass marketing envelopes, which one did you open first? Few people take the time to do this, which is why a handwritten note stands out in a big way. I have established excellent professional relationships and friendships with people in this way.

How to Set the Stage for Opportunity—Organic & Targeted versus Carpet-Bombing & Time-Wasting

Ideally, your résumé is a leave-behind, not an introduction. While it's the most important document of your professional life and should be kept updated and in top shape for those moments when you need it, most opportunities will come your way through people you know, which is why it's so important to get to know people and let them get to know you.

The best opportunities are often organic and unexpected. That is, you've met someone who is a potential employer or client (or a lead to one) and bonded with him, impressed him enough to continue a conversation. You haven't worked hard on selling yourself because you've met in a casual context (at a party, in line at the grocery store, at a baseball game or wherever), but there is a connection and when he mentions he's a musician (or producer, post-house operator, runner at a studio, mixer, film editor, or insert any number of roles here), you ask a few relevant questions to open him up and get him talking.

So practice this formula, it uncovers oceans of opportunity:

1. Find out what the other person is interested in.
2. Try to direct the conversation with questions he will enjoy answering.
3. Then, LISTEN!

In the example above, any of the following are good open-ended questions to get (and keep) the conversation going:

☛ Where are you from? What brings you here?

☛ Who are your musical influences?

☛   What kind of music do you write/record/produce/prefer?

☛   Working on any interesting projects now? Tell me about them!

From the answers to your questions may come more questions, and it may soon become appropriate for you to mention your audio skills. Ask to hear some of the person's material (or the project he's working on), show a sincere interest. Be sure to get *his* contact details (don't rely on him to follow up with you) and give him yours. Check his music/project out, and ask to come down to the studio.

Take it from there.

Organic, naturally occurring situations like this are more effective than blind mailing of résumés and cover letters to people you don't know, whose needs you don't understand, and who don't care because they're busy with their own work and challenges. It's through asking questions that you find out what the person's real needs are—which helps you understand if you're in a position to help. Voila! You then step in as the solution to his challenges!

COACH'S CORNER: Music Placement Opportunities

I came upon two recent opportunities quite organically to place music in a film and a TV show. Music placement in film and TV has become intensely competitive, and without great contacts it's almost impossible to get a response to an inquiry, much less an opportunity to pitch and place music. And yet these two opportunities fell into my lap because I was alert, listened and asked questions.

The first occurred in line at a grocery store. The man ahead of me was talking loudly on his phone (which I loathe in public places). With no option but to listen, I tuned in to what he was saying. He was discussing music in a project he was working on. When he finally got off the phone, I engaged him in conversation. "Sounds like you're busy!" I offered, and the conversation started. It ended with me getting his card and a description of the type of music he needed for a documentary he was working on.

The second scenario happened on the shuttle from the plane to the terminal at JFK International airport in NYC. Again, I was subjected to a loud conversation of someone seated next to me and again, I couldn't help overhear that the exchange was all about a television show in production. I heard enough to follow this person when we arrived at the terminal, all the way to baggage claim until she finally got off the phone. I opened with, "Sounds like quite a project you're working on!" and this led to me meeting the producer of a television show in production. Yes, she needed music. And I offered to help.

As I said, opportunity is everywhere.

Ask Questions. Listen.

Imitate Socrates. Questions are the most effective way to find out what people want or need. Inquire rather than talk. Show that you respect the other person's point of view.

After you've asked a question, practice silence and learn to *listen*. Show the other person that you are sincerely interested in what he says. Give him the attention and appreciation that he craves but rarely gets. Listen with enthusiasm! To be a good conversationalist, remember:

"The wit of conversation consists more in finding it in others, than showing a great deal yourself."—Benjamin Franklin

If you're shy, it's an easy way to shift the talking to someone else. And if you're shy, it's no crime. I was once shy, too. I got over it when I realized how much of life and its adventures were passing me by.

So let's get to the creation of your résumé. The guidelines in the following chapter will help you create an airtight résumé.

Your Marketing Tools—the Résumé

Creating Your Résumé Checklist

Here is a checklist you can use to create a résumé or polish up one you already have, with sample résumés below.

Three Versions

I recommend you create three versions:

The Short Résumé (samples on pages 94-97) should be only one page long. If you can't get someone's attention with one page, you won't get it with two. Your short résumé should be constantly modified and adapted to specific jobs for which you apply, and it contains your best benefits, skills and features to future employers.

Your Text-Only Résumé is important because many companies have firewalls and filters in place, which can snag or scramble an attachment. Always paste a text-only version of your résumé into the body of an e-mail in addition to sending an appropriately formatted version as an attachment (your short version). Send your text-only version to yourself first to test and make sure it looks good on the receiving end.

Your Master Résumé contains every job (dating back to your first paper route!), skill, accolade, award, civic duty, sport, activity, volunteer assignment you've ever had, it can be many pages long. This is for your reference only, and is important to keep updated so you can cherry-pick the best and most relevant aspects of your professional experience for each specific job for which you apply. Keep a file folder and include post-it notes, awards, articles, testimonials, words of praise from clients or employers, notice of promotions, job descriptions and the like in this folder. When these materials are kept current, you'll have less of a scramble when you want to apply for a new opportunity.

Presentation

No Typos: Goes without saying, doesn't it? Then why do employers get so many résumés with typos, when they're so easy to fix? Even one typo in a résumé or cover letter is too many for me, and I toss such documents immediately. Your résumé and cover letter are the most important documents of your career. If you are sloppy with them, what hope do I have that you will give my documents better care if I hire you? None! Proofread, or have someone you trust proofread for you.

No Templates: Templates often make poor use of space and shaded boxes, and are generally poorly organized. No template accommodates all users and levels of experience.

No Shaded Boxes: These transmit poorly via fax and e-mail. They serve no purpose that cannot be accomplished with bold-face or italic type, and they can snag your transmission (or botch it entirely).

Fonts: Use clean fonts such as Helvetica, New Century Schoolbook or Times New Roman. Avoid strange, small or wacky fonts or graphics unless you're a graphic artist. Even then, your résumé should be clean and neat without overbearing or distracting design. Use 11-point font minimum. Anything smaller is difficult to read, especially after it has been copied or faxed.

Paper: Use good quality white paper if you must print it. Invest in a higher-grade stock and get matching envelopes. Plain white high-grade paper is fine. Even though we are ruled by e-mail today, for that reason alone it's wise to use good old snail mail to follow up (see more on Transmissions below). Don't use colored paper, this transmits and copies poorly.

Printing: Use a quality laser printer and make clean copies on high quality white paper. If you do not have access to a decent laser printer, check your local library, university or Kinkos.

Order: Unless there is good reason to do otherwise (occasionally there is), list jobs you've held in chronological order with your most recent position first. Emphasize the most relevant aspects of your experience that pertain to the position for which you apply, placing these first or within each job description, depending upon which position you apply for. This order may change with each job for which you apply. It's useful to get a copy of your job description from your employer when hired (including updates and new responsibilities whenever you're promoted). This helps you update your résumé for future use.

Length: The ideal length for your résumé is one page, more is unnecessary. Busy people won't read beyond one page. Exceptions may be made for professionals with 20+ years experience. Your résumé is a summary of your professional experience that is most relevant to the specific job for which you apply and should not include too much detail, just enough to pique the employer's interest and get a call and an interview. Less is more. Don't include letters of recommendation unless these are requested (but you should have copies of these with you every time you go to an interview in case they are requested).

Content

Your Résumé Should Include: Your résumé should include a Heading (your contact details), Objective (this is optional— see my notes below on advantages of *not* including an objective), Qualifications, Professional Experience and Education. Optional categories (if it's relevant and you can make space) include Skills, Honors and Academic Achievements, or simply Other (a catch-all). If you're a student without much experience and have some space to fill, you could include a short section for Activities, Sports or Special Interests.

The Heading: Do not include two addresses (school and permanent address), include your permanent address only. If you are a still a student, we want to de-emphasize that fact so listing a school address has the opposite effect. You don't want to remind employers of your student status. You're ready for the pro leagues!

The Objective: An objective could work for or against you, so consider carefully whether or not to include it each time you send out your résumé. Include an objective when you apply for a specific position that you can reference.

When *not* to include an objective: An objective stated on your résumé can pigeonhole you, which is the last thing you want. As a job seeker, you want to have as many options available to you as possible and not limit yourself by stating an objective that is more appropriately placed in a cover letter in any case.

For example, let's say your stated objective is "to secure a position in the sound design department at a major gaming company." And let's say your résumé ends up on the desk of a music supervisor or music clearance executive at a gaming (or other) company and, based on your skills, this exec sees you are qualified for a job in that other department. Upon seeing your narrow objective, however, he might never call you since you've expressed an interest in entering sound design specifically, rather than music supervision or music clearance. Both these areas are important and related, and would add much to your portfolio of knowledge and skills. Thus, an objective can work against you.

And take any interview, because one interview frequently leads to another (sooner or later) if you make a good impression on the first interviewer. He may not have a need for you at that moment, but would consider you for future openings. Plus, an interview is always a great opportunity to get more names of others who might be hiring, either within or outside the company. Executives refer good candidates to colleagues at other companies all the time.

Finally, everyone's objective is the same—to work hard and be recognized, so don't waste space saying it.

Success Stories—Problem, Solution, Result: When communicating to a potential client or employer, in person or in writing, summing up your success stories is powerful. Briefly describe the problem (disorganized filing system no one wanted to touch), the solution (you cleaned it up) and the result (cut document search time in half).

So instead of this:

Gopher errands and tasks, including delivering tapes, faxing, copying, filing, and phones.

... which is so boring and dull that I fall asleep while reading it, I would re-phrase it to show results, for example:

Example 1

Cleaned up previously disorganized filing system, which created much-needed space and cut document search time in half. Without waiting to be asked, I handled telephone overflow from departmental secretaries with heavy call volume to enable them more time on the phone with important clients. In so doing, I dealt with a number of customer complaints, 95% of which I was able to resolve satisfactorily, thereby lightening the load for my co-workers and increasing sales revenue as well as customer satisfaction.

Much more interesting, isn't it? This small story shows the applicant's initiative, team spirit, willingness to learn and contributions toward the bottom line, exactly what employers look for. And it provides facts instead of a boring list of hollow attributes that many people include in their résumés, which convey nothing. Ninety-five percent of all résumés include vague statements such as "team player" or "great communication skills," which are weak, while the second example above *demonstrates* these.

More than the specific job(s) you've had, this is the section in which you state in strong, proactive verbs what you've learned and accomplished that will benefit your future employer. Employers want to know what you can do for their company, not just that you have an audio engineering degree. Lots of people have that! Any person in a position to hire has problems to solve: too much work that's not getting done, a project on deadline, a company growing without enough staff to keep up with demands, a vacancy to fill by a recently departed employee, etc. The more specific you are and the better able you are to quantify results you've achieved that benefits the employer, the better.

Try these:

Example 2

As a runner at a busy recording studio, I arrived early every day and frequently worked overtime (unpaid) to accommodate the shifting needs of this high-traffic facility. I did everything from deliver master tapes to fetch sandwiches and help clean the main recording studios to enable faster turnaround for clients on deadline. On three occasions, I enabled clients to begin their mix *sessions earlier than scheduled. I created a filing system out of a mess no one wanted to touch, which took me two months, and discovered $1,785 in unpaid invoices owed to the studio, which was then collected. My filing system increased studio productivity and employee morale. Now people can find billing invoices and other accounting documents that they need immediately. The studio manager and several clients complimented me on my speed, efficiency and cheerfulness, and on my get-the-job-done attitude.*

Example 2 above says much more than the vague "team player" verbiage seen in a thousand résumés. This offers proof and *demonstrates* important qualities. This example is a small story rather than a disjointed list of vague qualities (such as team player, multi-tasker, problem-solver, etc.), which offer no evidence of the effect of your contributions.

Example 3
As an assistant, I acquired skills in all phases of music marketing, including promotion, viral Internet marketing, top Internet music sites, fan sites, best Internet digital distributors (including technical file specifications) and sales. Am able to identify and achieve specific goals, and lead a team. Created and implemented campaign for developing artist Suzy Q which resulted in 5,468 new "friends" on MySpace over a span of three weeks, four well-attended shows in Orange County (two sell-outs at Coach House and Sam's), dozens of positive blog mentions and sales of 2,500+ CDs.

Note how Example 3 quantifies each of the accomplishments of this applicant.

Example 4
As a retail associate, I acquired skills in inventory management, optimizing retail store space to increase sales, up-selling, store displays and customer service. Rated among top sales associates in the southwestern region, I increased my department's sales by 16% in 2008. Received high ratings in customer service and satisfaction from management and customers.

Note that qualifications described in example 4 are not all gained through experience at a recording studio, post house or music-related company—this is fine. List the skills you acquired that are valuable to employers everywhere: sales, inventory control, customer service, marketing, organization, etc.. These are valuable across many industries.

Skills: Obviously, in the audio engineering world, you will need to include your technical, programming and computer skills. But most important are your people skills, which I would also include. Great audio professionals know how to work with people, bring out the best in their artists and clients, diffuse tense and difficult situations, and work within budget. The greatest technician in the world will not go far without some people skills and understanding of how to soothe the savage beast that artists and clients can become.

No City, State, or Months of Employment (unless specifically relevant): These are generally superfluous.

No Months: Use only the years of your employment (correct: 1980–1985), not the months (incorrect: May 1980–June 1985). This is superfluous and takes up space.

Bullet Points: Don't use bullet points unless you have too little experience to fill a page comfortably. Otherwise, these take up too much room. And if you *must* use them, keep bullet point lists to three, five, or seven bullets (the ideal length, according to research).

Truth: Be sure all information is accurate. Stretching the truth can be okay within certain limits (such as saying you were an "assistant" instead of an "intern"). Many companies keep résumés on file for years and run cross-checks when they receive new ones. It's bad news if your old résumé on file doesn't correspond to the new one. Once lost, your integrity is irreplaceable.

Title: If your summer internship didn't have a title, give yourself one! Rather than listing yourself as an "intern," call yourself a "coordinator," "marketing assistant" or "sales associate."

Contact Information: Center your name, address, telephone number(s) and e-mail address at the top of the page in large, boldface type. Don't list two addresses (college and permanent)— use permanent address only. Also, don't list more than two phone numbers (home and cell) and one e-mail address.

Big Words: Don't use big words where small ones will do. Brevity and clarity are hallmarks of intelligence and good communication. Too often, people buy into the fallacy that using big words will make them sound more important and smarter than they really are. Avoid this—it doesn't work.

No Lengthy Eulogies: Keep your cover letter (or e-mail introduction) short and simple. Less is more. Busy people usually won't take the time to read long letters from people they don't know. Take a look at the sample cover letter shown later in this guide for an example of a short, direct cover letter to go along with your résumé. I use this template in proposals all the time.

Relevant Experience: Only include that experience which is most relevant to the position for which you apply—match your skills with the company's needs, borrowing language from the job description if possible. No need to include all your experience. Too much detail is not necessary except to add color and dimension. Remember that your résumé is merely a summary of your most relevant experience, just enough to pique the employer's interest and get an interview. However, do explain large gaps in employment (i.e., you were out of the country, caring for an ailing parent or relative, etc.).

GPA: This is unnecessary and can potentially undermine your efforts if too low or too high. Leave it out.

Quantify: Wherever possible, use quantitative accomplishment statements such as "more than tripled revenues in 1986 from $2 million to $6.1 million" or "surpassed annual sales quota three years in a row" or "saved studio $400 by negotiating equipment maintenance plan." Address *problems* faced in your previous jobs, the *actions* you took to solve these problems, and the *result* of your efforts. This will be an important part of your future job interviews.

Qualify: If you're unable to quantify your results, then use qualitative accomplishment statements that indicate results such as "increased productivity by improving worker morale and cutting down on employee sick leave" or "improved results" or "initiated intern program." If possible, at least estimate results in numbers.

TMI (Too Much Information): Do *not* include height, weight, marital status, hobbies or photo.

Cover Letter—No Frilly Sign-Offs: Don't use "very truly yours," "with kindest regards," or "warm regards." Stick with the simple "sincerely."

Proofreading and Grammar

No Articles (a, an, the): Your résumé need not be in complete sentences with subject, predicate, etc. Phrases are OK.

No Weak, Vague Verbs: Use strong, proactive verbs such as:

accounted for	improved
achieved	initiated
acquired	instructed
analyzed	invented
approved	justified
assembled	learned
authorized	maintained
collected	managed
compiled	organized
controlled	planned
created	profited
delegated	projected
demonstrated	regulated
designed	reported
determined	reviewed
developed	secured
directed	simplified
drafted	solved
earned	systemized
eliminated	strategized
engineered	supervised
established	tailored
estimated	trained
formed	transformed
headed	

No Verb Confusion: In present job, use present tense verbs. In all past jobs, use past tense verbs. Conform verb tenses.

No Passive Voice: Do not use the passive voice in your résumé or cover letter. Always use the more direct and powerful active voice. Wrong: "I am going to come to Los Angeles where I will be working in the record business." Much better: "I will move to Los Angeles and work in the record business."

Adverbs and Adjectives: Eliminate these, or keep to a bare minimum in your cover letter and résumé. This is more direct and saves space.

No Excessive Personal Pronouns (in résumé or cover letter): Be sure not to start too many sentences with "I" and avoid making general and unverifiable statements such as: "I am dedicated, prompt, great, wonderful, smart . . . and music is my passion . . ." This may all be true but it goes beyond the realm of fact and is meaningless to someone who doesn't know you. Stick to facts such as, "Having graduated in the top 5% of my class and interned at XXX company, I have acquired skills in all phases of music marketing including promotion, online sales, distribution and retail."

Tip: Focus on the company's—and employer's—needs and how you can help achieve these goals rather than on abstractions about yourself. Match your skills and experience with the needs of the employer.

Proper Nouns: "Internet" and "World Wide Web" (or "Web") are proper nouns and should always be capitalized. Also note the correct spelling industry terms such as SoundScan. It's one word, where the second "S" is also capitalized.

Random Capitalization Disease: Do you suffer from this contagious phenomenon? Many do. Don't arbitrarily capitalize words unless they are proper nouns.

Proofread and Edit Ruthlessly (two sets of eyes!): When you prepare an important document to send out such as a cover letter or résumé, it will benefit you to have a second set of eyes (another person) review it first. Ask for help! A fresh perspective can help catch typos, awkward wording or help put a better spin on your material. I consider myself a fairly decent editor and yet anything I send out is almost *always* improved by showing it to another person first. It's also useful to read your résumé and cover letter aloud. This will help you identify rough bits. Anything that sounds stilted (artificial or unnatural) when spoken should be edited for clarity.

Word Preference

No Clichés: Please don't use clichés or tired phrases. Use simple, fresh language.

CDs: Unless the CDs of which you speak actually own things, don't use possessive apostrophe (wrong: CD's).

Words of Death: This special category includes words and phrases you should avoid at all costs. Here are a few:

utilize	obtain
re-invent	attain
synergy	facets
handle	impact
unique	needless to say
on a daily basis	my bad
at this point in time	irregardless
nice	

COACH'S CORNER: Words That Have "Impact"

The word "impact" is so often misused that its misuse has become accepted. It is most often wrongly substituted for "affect." Example: "The impact of the water shortage on L.A. will be severe." This is incorrect. Impact means "to force tightly together; pack; wedge or it refers to a striking together; violent contact; collision; the force of a collision; or shock." The water shortage did not impact L.A., it affected L.A..

Miscellaneous Advice

No Opinions Please (state the facts, be bold and direct): Do not say: "I believe I could help your company increase its bottom line." Rather, "I will help your company increase its bottom line." This shows self-confidence and avoids superfluous language. Instead of "I think my experience would be a great asset to your company" go with this: "I look forward to an opportunity to demonstrate how my experience will be an asset to your company, and help you achieve your goals." Avoid "I think," "I believe" and other indirect language. Instead, use "I will," "I can" and "I am."

Transmission

No Mass Mailings: This is the lazy man's way out and nothing could be more useless and time-wasting to both the job seeker and potential employer(s). You will get far better results when you draft your cover letter and résumé with a specific recipient in mind or, as noted previously, you focus your efforts on building organic contacts. Identify specific companies at which you would like to work and research them. Find out who works there, get names of the executives in the specific departments in which you would like to work, their titles, direct telephone and fax numbers (if possible), e-mail, the name(s) of their assistant(s), etc. Target specific individuals. This requires time, thought, research and homework, which is why hardly anyone does it and why so few people get through. It's also the reason why the people that *do* the research *do* get through!

Each employer has needs, challenges and preferences. The only way to find out is to research, or just ask. Any letters addressed to "To Whom It May Concern" are generally discarded. This shotgun approach indicates the letter writer is (1) too lazy to find out to whom to address his letter; (2) doesn't care too much; and (3) has no one specifically with whom he can follow up. Personally, I would never hire the author of such a letter. It shows lack of initiative and attention to important details. The way you conduct your job search is a good indicator as to how you would conduct yourself as an employee if hired.

The Black Hole: The only exception to the rule to send correspondence general delivery (without a specific person's name) is if you run into the increasingly prevalent practice of applying online at a corporation's Website where no company personnel names are given (done deliberately, FYI). This is the "black hole keyword-searchable database nightmare" of job seekers, as well as being a blockade that companies put up to manage job-related inquiries, phone calls and emails (which can seriously eat into any busy human resource director's or hiring manager's time). In spite of this blockage, I would make every effort to track down the name of a human being to whom you can address your correspondence (in addition to sending it into the black hole) and then send your résumé to that person.

COACH'S CORNER: "A Funny Thing Happened on the Way to the Job Market . . ."

The Pizza Principle

This is the best hiring story I've heard to date. A young man was trying to get his foot in the door at an artist agency. Agencies are notorious for high turnover and long hours, but are a highly desirable place to launch a career in the music industry. For this reason, there are typically long lines of people—both young and not-so-young—trying to get in. This particular young man realized what he was up against, was getting no response, and did something daring and unusual. He ordered pizzas for delivery to the music agent he had targeted, taped his résumé to the pizza box and wrote on it with a sharpie, "Are you hungry? I am!" with an arrow pointing to his résumé. He got the job. This approach shows ingenuity, daring and creativity. No reason you can't do something like this as well. With a little research, you can even find out what your target's favorite food is!

Underdog Harvey Mason, Jr.

Producer/songwriter Harvey Mason, Jr., one half of the successful production team The Underdogs, told me a story about coming to Los Angeles to pursue his dream as a producer/songwriter. He found the hot spots, hung out at studios, met people. One day, he met a top producer and, eager to get this fellow his material, he tossed his demo tape into the back of the guy's convertible as he was pulling out of the parking lot. It worked! Be bold.

Federal Express

I know of a handful of instances in which entry-level and senior executive level positions have been filled by people who, following an interview, have Fed-Exed a thank you note together with a specific proposal or marketing plan to the executive who interviewed them. This requires research, good ideas, and an understanding of the company's (and interviewing executive's) problems and challenges. The clever applicant includes himself in this proposal or plan as the solution to the company's problem! Fed Exes are always delivered and opened immediately (unlike regular mail, which doesn't necessarily get immediate attention). Lastly, it communicates that this is important and that you're serious! Spend the extra $20 and get your materials on the right person's desk immediately. The way that you apply yourself to securing a job indicates a great deal about how you would conduct yourself in a job if it were offered to you. Smart employers know this and look for these indicators.

No Laziness: As mentioned earlier, you should modify your résumé for every position for which you apply. Every position is different and represents an opportunity to market your skills and services. Your research and the specific job description will help dictate modifications, which may be slight but meaningful. For example, use text from the specific job description in your résumé and cover letter. Speak their language! If this sounds like too much work for you, are you sure you really want a job?

E-mail: Do not use a company e-mail account to send your résumés out to another company and potential employer, and use a private e-mail address on your résumé. Your e-mail address should be simple and include your name, such as Joe_Underwood@hotmail.com. In your correspondence, don't use e-mail addresses like "PimpMeNow@gmail.com" or "SugarBritches@hotmail.com" or anything unprofessional. Also, avoid cryptic e-mail addresses such as "CDTY8734@aol.com" or ones that are difficult for the recipient to remember and find in future. When someone decides to hire you and offer you a job, you want that person to be able to locate you! Cryptic e-mail addresses make this more difficult.

E-mailing Your Résumé: As many companies have firewalls and security measures in place that reject or scramble attachments, I suggest you have a résumé version to paste as a text-only version *into* the body of your e-mail. Send it to yourself first to check for formatting issues on the receiving end. Also, be sure your attachment is a universally accepted format (such as PDF) or whatever type of document the employer specifies. Someone who doesn't follow this simple direction puts himself in the wrong pile! As an attachment, the title of your résumé document should include your name, for example, "Joe_Underwood_Résumé.doc" as opposed to "Résumé.doc" or anything generic. Once your document arrives in the employer's office, he needs to be able to file and retrieve it easily. Anyone responsible for filling a position probably has dozens (if not hundreds) of such documents to sift through. Make yours easy to file and retrieve.

CHAPTER 7

Sample Résumés and Cover Letters

Getting Started

In the résumé *before* and *after* samples shown in this chapter—figures 7 through 10 (before, and then after versions of each) respectively—I have re-done two résumés: one of a recent audio engineering graduate and one of student with little more than internship experience.

In both cases, I have de-emphasized the fact that they are recent graduates by placing their education at the bottom of the page and highlighting qualifications at the top. Why? Because students with little or no experience in the workforce face two obstacles: first, they will be competing with many more seasoned professionals and second, lack of experience may be a deterrent to getting hired—a lovely Catch-22. What can you do? If you are in this position, the answer is to emphasize your qualifications and minimize (de-emphasize) the fact that you are a recent grad.

A Sample Cover Letter

A cover letter is more than a quick note to accompany your résumé. It's essential that it be well written and professional, which is exactly the impression you want to make with potential employers.

The following sample cover letter has been adapted from an original, which appears in Dale Carnegie's *How to Win Friends and Influence People*. It's one of the best I've ever seen. It's short, direct, and tells the recipient what the candidate has to offer rather than merely asking for a job.

March 15, 2010

Mr. Joe Anderson
TITLE [insert title here]
COMPANY [insert full company name here]
ADDRESS
ADDRESS

       Re: Opportunities at COMPANY [insert company name here]

Dear Mr. Anderson:

My five years of audio engineering experience should be of interest to a rapidly growing production company like yours.

In various capacities in studio operations with Pyramind in San Francisco, leading to my present assignment as assistant engineer and marketing manager, I have acquired skills in all phases of audio engineering, including mixing, sound design and production. Also, I have contributed to Pyramind's revenue by recruiting/enrolling more than two dozen students and securing five clients for the company's pro-audio facilities.

I will relocate to New York in February and am sure I can contribute to your growth and profit. I will be in New York the week of January 3 and would appreciate the opportunity to show you how I can help your company meet its goals.

Sincerely,

Tony Corona

Enclosure: resume

Figure 6: *An example of an excellent cover letter.*

Joe Underwood
880 Folsom Street
San Francisco, CA 94107
Tel: 415-896-9800
Lil_Joe@gmail.com

Objective

- Highly experienced songwriter, composer and engineer seeking employment in field of sound recording, editing, arranging, producing and musical performance

Skills

- Expert Certification in Pro Tools 8, Pro Tools Certified Operator in Post-Production, proficient in Reason 4 and Ableton Live 7. Waves Certified. Proficient in Final Cut Studio and DVD Pro. Experience in planning and curating live music events.

Computer Skills:

- Complete knowledge MS PowerPoint, Word, Excel, proficient.

Work Experience

- **Composer, Songwriter, Remixer, Touring Musician, 2004-Present**
  Guitarist, vocalist in band Heavy. Released full length LP May 2007 which received critical praise.   Extensive touring locally and nationally. Responsible for booking and promoting shows. Catalog of remixes commissioned by Coughing Cat Records Label.

- **Composer, Zampagno Films/Stanford University Alumni Association, 2008-Present**
  Currently engaged with the Stanford University Alumni Association in creating a branding campaign titled YOUR STANFORDALUMNI.ORG. Responsible for scoring music forpromotional spots working closely with production team.

- **Producer, King River Creek Music and Arts Festival, July 2008**
  Responsible for producing two shows at Mission Creek Music Festival in San Francisco. Acted as liaison between artists and club owners. Supervised and delegated tasks to volunteers.

- **Composer, Underwood Productions, 2005-Present**
  Composed music for four short films all of which have been featured at periodical 48 Hour Film Festivals in San Francisco.

- **Mental Health Specialist/Relief Counselor/Diversity Trainer, Edgewood Center for Children and Families, 2006-Present**
  Provide the therapeutic component for emotionally disturbed youth with a multidisciplinary team.   Led daily Art Therapy and social skills groups with students. Developed, implemented and currently   teach Cultural Diversity Training to new hires.

Education
- **Pyramind**, San Francisco, CA
  Digital Sound Producer - Complete Certification, December 2009

- **Eastern University**, St. Davids, PA
  BA, Double Major in Sociology and Urban Studies, Cum Laude, May 2002

References

Available Upon Request

Figure 7: *An sample résumé prior to following the "Tess Method" of presentation.*

Joe Underwood
880 Folsom Street • San Francisco, CA 94107
415-896-9800 • Joe_Underwood@gmail.com

SKILLS

Expert certification in Pro Tools 8, Pro Tools Certified Operator in Post-Production, proficient in Reason 4 and Ableton Live 7. Waves Certified. Proficient in Final Cut Studio and DVD Pro. Experienced in planning, curating, and producing live music events. Complete knowledge of MS PowerPoint, Word, and Excel.

PROFESSIONAL

2004-Present   **Composer, Songwriter, Remixer, Touring Musician.** Guitarist, vocalist in band Heavy. Released full-length LP in 2007, which received critical praise. In consultation with band, drafted band agreement to clarify and agree on goals. Extensive touring regionally and nationally, routed band to save travel and hotel costs, increased revenue to group by negotiating with hotels (for reduced rates and free breakfast included with stay), club promoters (for higher fees and better terms) and others. Book and promote shows, adding shows to band's tour to capitalize on routing. Wrote marketing plan for band to put us on track to record next album, perform locally and tour again. Help design and create merch to sell at shows and increase revenue to band. Catalog of remixes commissioned by Coughing Cat Records. Created remixes per label specs, delivered them on time and under-budget for 9% savings to label.

2008-Present   **ORGANIC FILMS / STANFORD UNIVERSITY ALUMNI ASSOCIATION, Composer.** Engaged with Stanford University Alumni Association to create branding campaign entitled YOURSTANFORDALUMNI.ORG. Scored music for promotional spots and worked closely with production team.

July 2008   **KING RIVER CREEK MUSIC & ARTS FESTIVAL, Producer.** Produced two shows at King River Creek Music Festival in San Francisco. Liaison between artists and club owners. Based on my knowledge of local acts, selected talent ideal for festival patrons and maximum draw, which brought in record attendance. Supervised and delegated tasks to volunteers, created checklists to keep all team-members coordinated, hand-picked teams to handle difficult tasks.

2006-Present   **ALPINE CENTER FOR CHILDREN AND FAMILIES, Mental Health Specialist / Relief Counselor/Diversity Trainer.** Provide therapeutic component for emotionally disturbed youth with multidisciplinary team. Lead daily art therapy and social skills groups with students. A staff and client favorite, I was welcomed back after a vacation with handmade cards by youth clientele who missed me. Develop and teach Cultural Diversity Training to new hires.

2005-Present   **UNDERWOOD PRODUCTIONS, Producer.** Composed music for four short films. All were featured at 48 Hour Film Festivals in San Francisco. Learned how to do step-deals (deferred payment), negotiated all deals, administered all clearances.

EDUCATION

2009   Pyramind, San Francisco, CA. Digital Producer
2002   Boston University, Boston, MA. Bachelor of Arts, Double Major, Sociology & Music, Cum Laude

Figure 8: *A sample résumé after following the "Tess Method" of presentation.*

JANE COOL - SAMPLE RESUME
123 Walnut Place, Granada Hills, CA 91344 (818) 555-1212 lil-jane@aol.com

OBJECTIVE:
A full time position in the Music Industry.
EDUCATION:
University of California Los Angeles   September 2001
BA in Sociology, Minor in Psychology, GPA 3.4
QUALIFICATIONS:
  *Hardworking and reliable.
  * Strong organization skills.
  * Ability to multitask in a fast paced environment.
  *Computer Literate: Microsoft Office (Word, Excel), Windows, Soundscan.
  *Excellent verbal and written communication skills; typing skills: 45WPM.

INTERNSHIP EXPERIECE:
  PUBLICITY INTERN
  Weissman/Delson Communications, N. Hollywood, California   May 2001- Sept. 2001
  *Assist publicists in various functions: transcriptions, data entry, research, preparations
of promotional and publicity packages, clerical functions.

PROMOTIONS AND PUBLICITY INTERN
Atlantic Records, Los Angeles, California   April 2000-June 2000
  *Prepared promotional packages, mailings, researched information, faxing, filing.

VOLUNTEER INTERN
Nsoul Records, North Hollywood California   July 1999-Sept. 1999
  *Assisted in various departments; prepared promotional packages, researched
information, aided in organizing events/CD release parties, faxing, filing, phones.

A&R INTERN
Arista Records, Santa Monica, California   April 1999-June 1999
  *Report to A&R VP/Supervisor; listen and evaluate demos; maintain computer
database log of demo submissions; look up information on Soundscan; write and
track response letters; research bands and industry events; answer multiple phone lines
for A&R department; provide submission information to musicians; faxing and filing.
WORK EXPERIENCE:
  ADMINISTRATIVE ASSISTANT
  YMCA, Santa Monica, California   July 1999- Sept. 1999
  *Assisted with various duties; data entry, bookkeeping, time cards, end of shift
information, faxing, filing, answering phones.
HONORS AND ACTIVITIES:
  *National Society of Collegiate Scholars.
  * Program Coordinator for Armenian Tutorial Project.
  **Who's Who Among High School Americans and The Dean's List*.
                      *Awaken A Cappella.

Figure 9: *A sample résumé (#2) prior to following the "Tess Method" of presentation.*

JANE COOL - SAMPLE RESUME
123 Walnut Place, Granada Hills, CA 91344
Tel: (818) 555-1212, jane_cool@aol.com

QUALIFICATIONS

Acquired knowledge of who's who (including music directors, program directors and other personnel) at Top 40, Triple A and country radio stations in primary, secondary and tertiary markets in the U.S. by creating nationwide database. Understand how to create regional and national media buying campaigns. Able to diffuse tense situations with difficult personalities.

PROFESSIONAL

2001   **WEISSMAN/DELSON COMMUNICATIONS, Publicity Assistant.** Assist publicists with transcriptions, data entry, media research, preparation of promotional and publicity packages. Took overflow work from staff secretaries.

2000   **ATLANTIC RECORDS, Promotions & Publicity Assistant.** Prepared and mailed promotional packages; researched radio stations in primary, secondary and tertiary markets, including personnel such as program and music directors, music formats and submission requirements; created nationwide database of radio station personnel, which cut down on search time.

1999   **NSOUL RECORDS, Assistant.** Prepared and mailed promotional packages; researched radio stations in primary, secondary and tertiary markets. Organized and coordinated events such as CD release parties, researched caterers to find best deals and negotiate costs, saving several thousand dollars.

1999   **ARISTA RECORDS, A&R.** Reported to VP of A&R. Listened to and evaluated demos, maintained computer database log of demo submissions, tracked weekly sales information on SoundScan, wrote and tracked response letters, researched bands and industry events, answered multiple phone lines for A&R department, provided submission information to musicians.

SKILLS   Microsoft Office, SoundScan, 45 wpm, excellent verbal and written skills

HONORS AND ACTIVITIES

National Society of Collegiate Scholars, Program Coordinator for Armenian Tutorial Project, Who's Who Among High School Americans and The Dean's List, Awaken A Cappella

EDUCATION

2001   University of California Los Angeles, BA in Sociology, Minor in Psychology

Figure 10: *A sample résumé (#2) after following the "Tess Method" of presentation.*

8

You, the Complete Package

The Elevator Pitch

The so-called *elevator pitch* gets its name from a scenario in which you find yourself alone in an elevator with Mr. Big, who is your captive audience for about 30 seconds, or until the elevator reaches his floor. This is your 30-second shot to get his attention and pitch yourself to him.

Often, you'll find yourself unexpectedly standing right next to someone who could have a huge and immediate affect on your career. So what do you say? What is your goal? Can you articulate it to yourself and to Mr. Big? And can you express it to him in such a way that captures his attention and gets him interested enough to invite you to call, follow-up or drop by? Or hire you? Or refer you to his colleague, Mr. Bigger?

Opportunities like this occur constantly, so be prepared, even when not speaking to a Mr. Big. You never know to whom you're talking, or whom he knows. Every time you meet someone, especially someone in your field of interest, it's an opportunity. When that person says "tell me about yourself," you should come back with a polished, focused 10 to 30-second elevator pitch, something like this:

"I've got four years experience in audio engineering, but my strength is live recording. I work well in chaotic situations with challenging personalities, and know how to bring out the best in artists. I've worked with X, Y and Z production companies, and I'm looking for something in this area."

Or this:

"I've just graduated with a music production certificate from Pyramind, I have two years experience in video game sound design and am a big gamer myself. I know the best games out right now, who's buying them, and how to create sound for them. I've tested my sound creations at local clubs where I deejay and have gotten rave reviews and requests for demos. I'm looking for an opportunity at a major gaming company in Los Angeles or New York, but am willing to relocate anywhere."

If you can't articulate this to yourself, work on it—rehearse in front of your mirror, friends, or family until it's smooth and polished. Friends and family can offer useful suggestions and feedback. Then start spreading the word and let others know, too.

Make it short and snappy where it can be modified to fit a particular circumstance. If you wheel out the equivalent of Tolstoy's *The Brothers Karamazov* (too long!), you'll lose Mr. Big's attention and your opportunity.

References, Referrals, Testimonials Letters of Recommendation

Buyers (read: potential clients or employers) demand social proof, that is, evidence that you've got the skills and ability to perform a job. That's why there is nothing more effective to sell you to the buyer than a previous happy client or employer. The best way to get this proof is—you guessed it—just ask!

References: References are former employers, supervisors, co-workers, clients, and others whom you have impressed in the past with good work. As noted in the Résumé Checklist section, you should have these but I recommend against including their names and contact details in your résumé unless specifically requested. Better to provide your list of references only on request so that those people who vouch for you will only receive calls from serious employers.

When you're up for a job, it's smart to call each reference to let them know about it, to remind them that they may receive a call and, in fact, to encourage them to call the potential employer/client on your behalf and put in a good word.

Referrals: Not to be confused with references above, referrals are people whom others introduce to you, suggest you call or get in touch with.

Discuss your plans with others, especially the supporters in your inner circle and on your team, and don't forget family and friends. Just because they're not in "the business" doesn't mean they don't know someone who is, so make your dreams and ambitions known. Everyone knows someone, and folks love to feel as if they're helping. Many good referrals can come your way with this simple strategy, especially if you're open, a good listener, and ask questions.

COACH'S CORNER: The Continuing Referral

Don't be shy about asking for more names from people who can give you referrals. Be sure to get permission to use their name, so you can say: "Hi, Mr. Jones, my name is Joe Underwood and I'm referred to you by George Smith at Prime Time Studios who suggested I call you." It is helpful to record where and when you met the person, birthdays, and any unusual or interesting information that will help you remember this person. In particular, pay attention to your new contact's likes and dislikes . . . This is a useful hook with which to maintain meaningful communication and help create a favorable opportunity to submit yourself—and your résumé—for a position.

If you get through to Mr. Jones, whether or not he is receptive to your overture, be sure to report back to George Smith at Prime Time Studios who gave you this valuable contact in the first place and let him know what's happening (i.e., that you managed to speak with Mr. Jones for a few minutes, that you've scheduled a meeting with him, or whatever). This keeps George invested in the process—and progress—and demonstrates that you are grateful for his help and referral. The result? Show gratitude and you're likely to get more of this valuable gift: more referrals and more help toward your goal (landing a great job).

Again, it's about creating relationships and being human. Making and having human contact is so much more effective than submitting your résumé into the black hole of a corporate Website with a keyword searchable database.

Being able to call someone you don't know and say 'I was referred by our mutual friend Joe' strengthens your position and hugely tilts the odds in your favor of receiving a favorable response. Why? Because people feel a strong sense of obligation to friends and professional colleagues and don't want to look bad or get in trouble for not responding. If a friend or colleague referred you, then you must carry some importance, or why would this mutual friend have referred you in the first place?

We know if a friend or colleague thought we are important enough to think of and he refers third parties to us, we preserve our standing in his eyes by being responsive to requests. *Referrals work*, so be sure when you are referred by someone that you immediately announce this, put it up front in a voice mail message (or in a communication to a receptionist of secretary) or in the subject line of your e-mail. Don't bury it in your communication.

Examples of how to use a referral for maximum benefit:

1. In a voicemail: "Hello Mr. Jones, I'm referred to you by [mutual friend] George Smith, and my name is Joe Underwood. My number is 818-555-1234. George recommended that I call you about how I can help you and your company meet your goals because of my experience in XXX. I would appreciate an opportunity to speak with you. Once again, my number is 818-555-1234. Thank you."

2. In an e-mail: Subject line: Referred by George Smith. Body of message: Dear Mr. Jones: I am referred to you by mutual friend] George Smith. He recommended that I call you about how I can help you and your company meet your goals because of my experience in XXX. My number is 818-555-1234 and I would appreciate an opportunity to speak with you. Once again, my number is 818-555-1234. Thank you.

3. When leaving a message with a receptionist or secretary: "Hi there, this is Joe Underwood for Mr. Jones, I'm referred to him by George Smith. And to whom am I speaking please?" Always get the secretary's name and make a note of it—you'll want to be on good terms with all the gatekeepers!

You must reach out to people, no matter how remote or out of reach they may seem. *Everybody* knows somebody, and most people are happy to help open doors and make introductions for you when they can—it makes them feel important and good about themselves.

Testimonials: Anytime anyone says something great about you, capture it in writing, whether you make notes yourself and put it in your master résumé file, print out a copy of the glowing e-mail or create a document to include these kind words. Some Websites (such as Linked-In.com) have modules that enable solicitation and publication of testimonials, and you can use these or do it yourself. Don't be shy to solicit good words from people for whom you have performed well. Ask! These can be excerpted in your résumé, cover letter, on your Website or just mentioned in an interview.

Letters of Recommendation: Also important to have in your master résumé file to pull out when needed. If you don't have any letters of recommendation, ask for them and offer to draft a letter to help speed the process.

Business Cards & Database

Business Card Business cards are easy and inexpensive to print, and they make a statement: You're a professional! Having a professional-looking business card and handing it to someone you meet sends a signal—you're not some guy who has to scratch his name on a cocktail napkin or paper plate—and handing yours to someone makes it easier to get theirs.

I recommend printing one all-purpose business card (you can have alternative versions if you like for different occasions) to include your name, e-mail and phone number on good quality white stock. Include your address if permanent, and if not just leave it off. Super simple:

Joe Underwood
Joe_Underwood@gmail.com
818-555-1234

I recommend against including much more detail than that because if you have a variety of skills, you don't want to be pigeon-holed or dismissed if your card says "Live Event Audio Expert" but a studio gig comes up which you'd be equally qualified to work. Including something general like "Audio" would be OK, but keeping it simple enables you to listen to the needs of the prospective client and then become what he needs! "It just so happens that I'm an expert in surround sound, etc." (only if you are, of course!).

Database: There is little point in collecting names, referrals and company contact details if you don't have a good way to organize them. Create a simple database system that works for you, and make sure to update it regularly and keep a backup. This could be as simple as a spreadsheet, though there are many software programs available for just this purpose.

Because I meet so many people (and you will too), I include notes on where I met each person and/or who referred me to him. Linking the new person to an event or someone I already know helps me to remember him. Free Web tools like freecrm .com allow you to keep detailed notes and contact information available 24/7 online, including birthdays and special information that helps keep the contact human and personal.

COACH'S CORNER: Keeping Business and Pleasure Separate

You'll find plenty of free online tools to help you manage your network, from social sites like Facebook and MySpace to LinkedIn and others. Be careful how you mix your professional and your personal online profiles though. The Wall Street Journal carried a front-page story in early 2009 about a Harvard graduate who posted his MySpace page on his résumé. He then posted drunken photos of himself at graduation on this page, turning off employers who passed on him for several opportunities—each worth over $150,000 per year!

Your Network

Establishing connections, then staying in touch to create a strong professional network, is an essential component of success in any professional environment, especially in the entertainment business. Here are some suggestions to help build yours.

If you're a student or recent grad, start with your teachers, school administrators and fellow students but don't forget the alumni roster of your school, and the career development center. Build your contact list from here. Also include your target list of companies. Other good sources for contacts are association meetings (civic and professional), industry conventions, club meetings, church or synagogue gatherings, or people you meet when you are out running errands or volunteering. In short, whenever and wherever you meet people, make it an opportunity to network.

Next, work the phones! Tell them what you're after and ask if they have any leads. Be proactive. When appropriate, send résumés with note of thanks (or cover letter) to primary contacts and be sure to follow up. Where secondary contacts are concerned, follow up your correspondence by suggesting coffee, lunch or a breakfast meeting. Get involved: volunteer at some association functions and offer to help organize these events, etc.

Use your contacts wisely and properly. Help keep their attention focused on you, on your individual skills and accomplishments, and how potential employers might use your experience. Always remember to offer your assistance to your contacts in any way possible and if they do ask a return favor—honor it. No one likes doing favors for people that won't return them.

Always ask permission to use the name of a contact, then use it in correspondence and phone conversations. Nothing gets you inside the castle walls more quickly than a personal reference. Always open your communication with a phrase such as "I am referred to you by John Smith, who suggested that I contact you." Make your correspondence brief, ending with a proactive statement about calling or visiting soon to discuss mutually beneficial ideas.

Then, follow up. After each communication, ask when would be a good time to follow up with the potential employer or contact. Then do it in the time frame specified (good idea: get a personal organizer or calendar now to keep track of these things). Report back with any success stories to your original contact. This keeps him informed, and gets him more invested in you and creates psychological leverage for you.

Your network will work for you but you must cultivate and grow it. When you research potential employers and companies, add them to your database. When you meet new people who may be able to help you in your job search (which could include almost anyone), ask for a business card and take time periodically to input this information in your database and create an easily accessible system. Everyone is fair game: your hairdresser or barber, hockey coach, grocer, or next-door neighbor. Don't forget other students, alumni, teachers and professors, and the folks in the career center at your school. Happy clients are great sources of referrals, too, or any one you've managed to impress. For those already out in the working world, this includes co-workers, supervisors and subordinates, your counterparts at other companies, and folks whom you've met through work.

You'd be surprised how many connections will appear effortlessly if you just speak up, be friendly and ask. Learn good people skills—this is vital. With good people skills, you can get through to anyone. The key is to treat people as you yourself wish to be treated and not as springboards to be used and discarded. Contact them personally, with respect, and show that you've done some homework. Show them you know their work, admire what they have accomplished and would appreciate an opportunity to work alongside them and add value.

In the case of potential employers, identify a few individuals at the company where you wish to work and quasi-stalk them. That is, research them intensely, learn their habits, preferences, professional role where they work, find out the name and preferences of their receptionist and assistant, find out where they eat so you can "bump into them" in the valet parking line at their favorite restaurant, know their company and projects intimately, etc. Getting to know the gatekeepers is a great way to get to know the boss.

Most important of all, seek ways to help others. Make it about them, not about you. When you've created a relationship, you're in a better position to ask for help, or a job or whatever you need. You've established credibility, paved the way by making yourself valuable, respected, and known, and by demonstrating that you're not just one more person sending out hundreds of résumés.

Attributes of Winners & Losers

Clearly you need to include technical skills in your résumé such as audio, computer and sound design programs, gear you're familiar with, etc. I recommend including a few "soft" skills, too. The most brilliant technicians don't get far unless they have good people skills. With more students graduating from engineering schools, most people will have basic skills. If you have some of the attributes below, you will be ahead of the pack.

How many of the following describe you?

Attributes of Winners

All of these can be developed or learned.

Ability to overcome resistance

Ability to overcome shyness, fear and intimidation

Ability to remember names

Acts like a professional

Active (not passive)

Charisma

Consistency

Courage and conviction. Those who don't take risks work for those who do.

Creativity

Curiosity

Decisiveness

Discipline

Expect more

Flexibility

Focus

Follow-up

Friendliness, ability to build rapport with people

Generosity

Goal-orientation

Good manners and etiquette

Gratitude and appreciation

Honesty

Humor

Imagination

Initiative

Knowing when to let go

Listening

Not taking yourself too seriously

Positive energy, enthusiasm and optimism

Punctuality

Smiling and eye contact

Takes responsibility

Trust in yourself and your instincts

Attributes of Losers

Most of these are within your control. How many of these describe you? Is it time to make some changes?

"What's in it for me?" attitude

Bad jokes

Doesn't take risks

Fear

Inability to communicate qualifications

Interrupting

Irresponsibility

Lack of confidence

Lack of involvement

Limited presentation of skills and abilities

Narcissism

Obedience

Passivity

Poor appearance and demeanor

Profanity

Settling

Shyness

Sloppiness

Smoking (when meeting someone new)

Talking too much, talking too little, not listening

"Being good in business is the most fascinating kind of art. Making money is art and working is art and good business is the best art."
—Andy Warhol, artist/filmmaker/social icon

Getting In: Give to Get

This simple concept will set you apart and make people more responsive to you, happy to return your phone call or take a meeting with you. Take a sincere interest in what motivates people and in what they want. Consider what you can offer them instead of asking what they can do for you. What value can you bring to the table? How can you help the person whom you wish to approach achieve his/her goals?

This strategy works brilliantly because you're providing useful, valuable information and resources to your prospective employers and clients. You spend virtually no time talking about what you do or what you know. Instead you learn about what *they* need and determine where *they* want to go. And now, instead of pushing people away, they are attracted in droves because you have something they want—the promise of a solution that works.

Now when you attend networking events, the focus and purpose are completely different. You don't talk about yourself, you ask questions and listen. You don't give out your résumé, demo or card urging people to call, you ask for their card and tell them you'll send them a recent article you've written (or read), tickets to a show, music or a case study of a successful project. You do contact past clients, but it's rarely to ask for work, it's more often to share an idea or a resource. But your call is never a voice from the past, because these people have been getting your newsletter or eZine every month for the past year. They're happy to hear from you. And when you mail letters to many prospects, it's not to ask for business or a job but to invite them to an event or tell them about a valuable report you'd be happy to send, or something that will interest them personally.

CHAPTER 9

Setting the Stage for Opportunity

Etiquette, Professional Protocol & How to Work the Telephone

Walking up to people you don't know, introducing yourself and thrusting a résumé (or tape or script) into their hands is extremely poor form.

In most cases, the appropriate course of action—which will increase your odds of achieving your objective—is to introduce yourself, chat briefly, and then request a business card. Engage, ask questions, listen! Feel free to ask if your target would mind if you called later with a few questions or send your résumé because you're very interested in his particular area of work, etc. Try to make a personal connection before you do this, otherwise this person won't remember you. When following up, be sure to include a short note referencing when and where you met this person.

Telephone Etiquette

Be brief and courteous. Get the name of the person who handles incoming calls because chances are good you'll speak to him again soon. It pays to be courteous to the gatekeepers. Be sure to put the assistant's name in your growing database! Some good opening lines:

"Hello, my name is Joe Underwood. May I please speak to George Brown?"

The assistant will ask what this is regarding. Tell him and be brief. Also, "May I get your name please?"

And, of course, "Thank you very much for your help Mike (assistant's name), I appreciate it."

Use the assistant's name—this helps establish a personal connection. Saying the assistant's name will help you remember it, and it also (consciously and subconsciously) let's Mike know that she's been identified and will be held accountable for delivering your message.

After you've called several times, "Hi, Mike (assistant's name), this is Joe Underwood for George Brown, is he available please?"

If Mike won't let you through and you have to leave a voice-mail, leave brief, clearly spoken messages. Repeat your number twice *s-l-o-w-l-y, once at the beginning and then again at the end of your message*. For example:

"Hi Mr. Brown, this is Joe Underwood calling to follow up on the résumé and letter I mailed you last week regarding the position as an intern in your department advertised on your Website. Please call me at your convenience at (818) 555-1234. I am very interested in working with you. I have all the necessary qualifications, and more. I am prepared to begin immediately. Again my number is (8 1 8) 5 5 5—1 2 3 4 (spaces denote slight pauses). I look forward to hearing from you soon. Thank you."

Do NOT leave more than one telephone number except with good reason—it's just plain annoying. Do they expect anyone, especially a busy person, to take down all those numbers and call them all?

COACH'S CORNER: Getting Past the Gatekeeper

If getting through to the top executive is difficult, try calling after hours. Many execs will pick up the phone before their assistant arrives or after he/she leaves for the day. If you get the exec on the phone, be prepared, polite and direct.

Be sure the outgoing message on your answering machine or voice mail service is polite, clear, and succinct if you expect calls from potential clients or employers. Also, if you do not have a dedicated telephone line, be sure to secure a backup system or voicemail service, so that a person calling does not receive a busy signal because you're on the Internet, etc. Be sure you're able to receive any call that comes in—busy people are not likely to phone twice, and you'd hate to miss an opportunity!

Ten Reasons Why Phone Calls *Aren't* Returned

1. Your message is vague and cryptic. Be clear and specific. Rehearse!
2. No call-back number.
3. Your call-back number is too difficult to hear. State your number clearly at the beginning *and* at the end of your message. Do not leave a message or make a call with a symphony of background sound in your environment such as eating, chewing, traffic, barking dogs, crying babies, whirring vacuum cleaners! Make your call in a quiet spot so you can focus and leave a clear message.
4. Remove distractions when making calls or leaving messages. Don't make lunch, check e-mail or run errands while doing this. Smile when you talk or leave a message—you can actually hear this!
5. Who are you? If referred by someone, state this up front. The value of the referral is when your target trusts the one who referred you as having his interest at heart, and that you're not calling to sell vacuum cleaners. Don't let the referring party down—explain why he thought the target would benefit from talking to you. Let the person [target] know your call will be brief.

6. You're cold-calling: everyone hates unsolicited sales calls—give the person a good reason to call you back.
7. You're rude to the gatekeeper.
8. You called at a bad or wrong time. Sometimes we don't need what's being offered at that moment.
9. You sound too needy and desperate. Sell yourself with confidence!
10. Some people prefer other modes of communication to the telephone. So ask!

Cold-Calling and Telemarketing Yourself

Create a Target List: Create a target list, pick up the phone and start calling. Don't overlook friends, family and business associates, even if they aren't in your chosen industry. In fact, start with them since all individuals have their own vast network—tap into them. No one should be safe from your phone calls (short of pestering, that is)! Call every company you've targeted, every department manager. Ask each person you talk to for suggestions of other companies or individuals who may be hiring. Even if the current lead goes nowhere, you can frequently get names and numbers of other targets. Research industry-specific and general business sources from which to pluck names.

COACH'S CORNER: Prepare for your calls

If you've targeted a list of ten companies to call on your job search, start cold-calling the bottom ones on your list. This will give you time and practice to improve your technique before you call the top companies on your list. Cold-calling is tough. It's so difficult that most people avoid it as a job search technique. It's easier to avoid, but this won't help your job search. In fact, this is dangerous to your career because you will miss out on many potential opportunities.

By networking, telemarketing, and cold-calling, you can access job leads better than your competition. Your momentum will build and you'll be busy and confident. Part of your technique is that if you get a rejection, you get off the phone quickly. You don't have time to waste. Chalk it up to their loss, move on to the next target on your list. There is a fine line between confidence and arrogance. Don't be rude. Don't be a pest. But believe that you have the skills and background to help that company. If it's not a good match, move on to the next target, but always be professional.

Telemarketing: Work the phone to find job leads. Start by calling friends and family. Develop your technique and if you're not getting results, review your technique. Don't keep repeating mistakes. Analyze what you say and the response you get. What works and what doesn't? Above all, listen! We tend to become preoccupied with what we say and with our own goals. Employers are not interested in your career trajectory; they're interested in filling needs or solving problems. Script a conversation, but don't fail to listen and respond to what the other person says.

Focus on improving, so when a call doesn't go well, use it as an opportunity to evaluate what you could have done better. Rest assured, many calls won't go well. Analyze your style and what you said and measure their reactions. You'll hear "no" a lot, but don't cave in quickly. Be flexible, attentive, and politely persistent!

Script Your Cold Calls: To help with your cold calls, prepare a simple script. Include the following elements:

1. Full name and title of the person you are calling.
2. The name of the person who referred you or the publication or source from which you got company's name.
3. Why you are calling—first, you want a job and second, you want more names if no job exists there.
4. How and why your qualifications match the needs of the person you are calling.
5. Your specific skills that are relevant to the job.
6. Why a personal meeting would be helpful to both you and the target. The incentive for the meeting may be an interest in your background, your industry or experience, the people you know, or ideas you can share. Propose several specific times, and be flexible.
7. Set a time limit Make your call clear and brief. Don't waste your target's time but be sure your time isn't wasted either (which is equally valuable).
8. Read and role-play your script with another person. Iron out the rough bits before you get on the line with an employer.

Keep accurate records of all of your calls and the responses— if there's a follow up call to make, be sure to make it!

COACH'S CORNER: Follow Through

As you make progress pursuing every lead, check back with the person who made the original referral that leads to any successful connection, call back, interview, job offer, etc. People who help you are rewarded when they know their suggestions and referrals have yielded fruit, and it is a mark of your professionalism to thank and update them. This process also psychologically bonds people to you and encourages them to invest in and continue assisting you with more referrals, ideas and contacts. And it's a great opportunity for a thank you note!

COACH'S CORNER: May I Help You, Sir?

The more helpful you are, the more likely people are to return your phone calls. After using the scripted points above, ask the people you're calling if they need help with anything. Listen and ask questions. To the degree that you are able to assist prospects in solving their problems, you become more valuable to them. Their "problems" may be viewed as your "opportunities." And by the way, when a client or employer makes an offer, reactivate all your cold-calling and telemarketing skills, find out what the market will bear and never accept the first offer.

Step Out of Your Comfort Zone—Take Risks!

Would you rather be comfortable or successful? One theory holds that you must be comfortable with discomfort to become (and remain) successful, that it's almost impossible to be both. I agree. This means you constantly have to step outside your comfort zone and overcome fear. The only time you grow is when you're uncomfortable.

"Courage is not the absence of fear, but the mastery of it."—Mark Twain, American author

Fear leads to shyness, paralysis and inaction— the road to nowhere. So you must overcome fear and not let it control you. How many opportunities and lives are squandered because of failure to address fear? Successful people constantly overcome their fears in order to learn and grow.

The benefits of working through your worst and mostly irrational fears are immense. Pushing beyond fear (and excuses) is essential to experience a full, rich life and to encounter opportunity and adventure. Facing your fears enables you to take risks. Falling down is normal and to be expected, but don't let it stop you from taking risks,. Don't retreat and don't make excuses, procrastinate or throw up obstacles in your own path or let others do this.

"Nothing will ever be attempted if all possible objections must first be overcome."—Samuel Johnson, poet, essayist, moralist, novelist, literary critic, biographer, editor, and lexicographer

"Every successful achievement begins with decision. Most unsuccessful lives are conspicuously absent of decision."—Dan Kennedy. The author of the **No B.S.** series of business and marketing books, Kennedy's texts are a must-read for everyone serious about marketing their business or skills.

Decide that you will succeed and be willing to take risks. The best opportunities come from taking risks. The universe loves stories of people who go out and put themselves in the path of opportunity. Taking risks means overcoming fear and working your way through it.

"Those who don't take risks work for those who do."—Alan Beck, President and founder of Pacific Concert Group and ITP Records

When you're a risk-taker, sometimes you get kicked. It always hurts, it never gets easier, and you're never immune to having someone stab you in the back or work around you. But you have to make it work to be successful.

"I try to act as if I make a difference."—William James, American psychologist and philosopher

COACH'S CORNER: Fake it 'till You Make it

Practice acting in spite of fear, inconvenience, and discomfort, and practice acting when you're not in the mood. This will build your confidence and soon taking risks will seem normal to you. And then be prepared for the flood of opportunity and adventures to come your way!

"Concerning all acts of initiative and creation, there is one elementary truth, the ignorance of which kills countless ideas and splendid plans: that the moment one definitely commits oneself, then providence moves, too. All sorts of things occur to help one that would not otherwise have occurred. A whole stream of events issues from the decision, raising in one's favor all manner of unforeseen incidents and meetings and material assistance which no man would have dreamed would come his way."—W.H. Murray, Scottish mountaineer in his book *The Story of Everest*

You must believe you are capable of achieving something before you achieve it. Failure to believe in yourself leads to self-sabotage and squandered efforts. Belief in yourself is a MUST—if you don't, who will?

"Whatever you can do, or dream you can, begin it. Boldness has genius, magic, and power in it. Begin it now."—Goethe, German poet and dramatist

Fear of the unknown for most people is the worst—we crave predictability and security. Becoming comfortable with uncertainty is the best thing you can do for yourself, which means becoming self-reliant. The world is chaos and you only have yourself to rely upon. If you are confident in your wits and skills, this will provide satisfaction and security. Let the world throw anything at you, you can handle it!

" . . . he knew full well the consequences of failure. That, of course, was the strength of men like him: they were not afraid to fail. The [sic] understood that the great accomplishments in history demands [sic] the greatest risks; that, indeed, history itself was shaped by the boldness, not only of collective action but of individual initiative. Those who panicked at the thought of failure, who did not act with clarity and determination when the moments of crisis were upon them, deserved the limitations to which their fears committed them."—Robert Ludlum, American author, from his book *The Parsifal Mosaic*

From School to the Real World

Make a Smooth Transition

If you're a student today, don't wait until the end of your senior year to start surveying the job market. By avoiding the last-minute scramble that your classmates experience, you can do many things to position yourself for a great job the minute you graduate.

The key is to view school or college as a laboratory. Most students don't realize what excellent access they have to resources and people, and fail to use it to their advantage until it's too late and they've graduated. Students also have a strong psychological advantage because society is conditioned to look favorably upon students. Because of this, a politely worded request or letter can go far, much farther than a similar request from someone already in the job market. Asking a busy executive for a job tends to illicit a different kind of [negative] response than asking to interview him for your school newspaper or senior project. Students are non-threatening, and are not suspected of corporate espionage or re-routed over to the human resources department. And so it behooves you to take full advantage of your student status and up the ante!

Here is just a sampling of things you can do while still in school that will help you narrow down your likes and dislikes, give you practical experience and position you much more favorably upon graduation. For the student interested in transitioning into the music business, consider the following ideas:

Teachers: Get to know your music and music business professors by talking to them before or after class, or during office hours. They can become your most valuable assets, mentors, and even friends. Find out what independent projects your professors are working on outside the classroom (research papers, performances, projects, businesses, etc.) and offer to help. Showing them your initiative and then following through will put you in a position to meet professionals on the outside. Getting to know them in this context is advantageous, especially if you perform brilliantly no matter how small the task you're given, which can lead to other introductions, letters of recommendations, being asked to work on more exciting projects and even—yes!—job offers.

Career Center: Visit the career center on campus and get to know the people there. Ask them about resources they can recommend about your industry or area(s) of interest, company profiles, articles, directories, etc.

Alumni Office: Visit the alumni office on campus and introduce yourself. Ask about alumni in your industry or area(s) of interest, get contact information, study up on them and reach out. Be sure to do your homework first before tapping into this excellent resource, and find creative ways to contact alumni, either to ask for advice, to invite them to speak at your college or university or to interview them for the school newspaper or a blog (perhaps your own blog that you start precisely for this purpose—see #9 below).

Project: Choose a record or music industry company you admire, do a term paper on it, analyze its successes and failures, market strengths and weaknesses. Use this opportunity to interview key executives at the company and others who can add insight, including those in the most humble positions, such as the mailroom. It has been my experience that the guys in the mailroom (it's usually guys) have great insight on many of the executives employed there and what's going at the company. And when the company is hiring!

Volunteer: Volunteer at a local concert promoter, indie label, recording studio, arts fair or summer music series in your area. If there isn't an event of interest to you, create one!

Start an On-Campus Recording Studio or Record Company: Network with professors and advisors, research successful studios and indie labels to use as a model and use this opportunity to interview executives at those companies. With creativity and persistence, you might even get the school to fund some or all of this. What an excellent way to learn the business!

Book Shows: Organize book shows on campus, or at a local library/community center, coffee house, or other venue. Consider doing house concerts! These shows will give you plenty of opportunity to practice audio skills live and meet interesting, talented and up-and-coming artists who can make excellent collaborators, leading to other opportunities and future work.

Create A Database: Compile data on local performers and artists, their music and how to reach them—such a resource can be immensely valuable especially if you start looking for acts to work with yourself.

The Power of Journalism (become a reporter!): As mentioned earlier, you will find much more resistance to asking for something (like a job) than you will when you offer something (like positive exposure or an interview). Becoming a reporter is your ticket to access. Everyone has an ego and most people love to talk about themselves. Use this fundamental aspect of human nature to your advantage. Interview local artists or executives for your campus newsletter or Website. Or start your own newsletter, Website or blog.

Radio: Interview local artists or executives for your campus radio show. If an appropriate program doesn't already exist, then create one.

Intern: Work part-time (as a volunteer or intern) at a recording studio, indie label or the regional branch of a major label or multinational company.

Local Artists: Work with a local artist you like to develop songs, a fan base, marketing plan, press kit and strategy. Produce their music, book and organize sound at shows, learn how to publicize and market artists to success.

Street Marketing Team: Tons of artists need to find and reach fans consistently. Start a street marketing team to help spread the word about artists you think are cool. You can identify the best ones to talk to about working in the studio, producing music, co-writing, etc.

Start a Club: Start an on-campus club in your area of interest: a general club for music-lovers, a fan club or a club for producers, DJs or folks interested in working in the business—you name it! Determine group activities and organize participants to execute them. Appoint yourself president, invite people who interest you to lecture to the group.

Abroad: Spend a year abroad and work at the regional branch of a multi-national corporation. This will garner great leads for you, especially if you learn a foreign language.

These are just a few ideas, there are many others. The key is to understand what an excellent environment a school or college campus is and how many resources are available to you if you simply ask or seek them out. Odds are the school may not have what you're thinking of and would love for you to take this project on! You have great latitude as a student, because you're not expected to know everything. Therefore missteps and failures along the way can be taken in stride much more easily than they would be in the real world where mistakes can get you fired. Use this cocoon, this laboratory-like environment to the fullest and experiment! You have plenty of support from teachers, counselors and advisors—it's their job to help you, but you must take the initiative and associated risks.

When you do, the rewards will be immense.

You will gain confidence in yourself and in your ability to make good decisions, you will build a valuable network of people around you (including other ambitious students) and find like-minded people. Your ability to speak to groups of people and lead them will grow, and this is such a tremendous asset. Any shyness you may have had before will become more and more a thing of the past, and you'll wonder how it was possible that you were ever shy in the first place. You will be able to determine at a much earlier age if the job you thought was cool really is or not, because you'll give yourself the opportunity to intern at the company of your dreams and see first-hand if it's all you imagined. Maybe it is, maybe it isn't, and maybe you'll find something else that you enjoy even more. All of this is great information and gives you a major head start in the competitive job market because you won't have to waste time at a job that's not right for you. You'll have a much better idea of what you enjoy, what you're good at and where you fit in.

All of these things are valuable springboards into the real world. If you work hard, follow-up and make those around you look good, you'll have job offers waiting for you on graduation (maybe even before your graduate!) and be in the position of having to choose the best of the bunch rather than scrambling for leftovers.

The power is yours. Take it, use it, do it!

Useful Skills to Help Get Your Foot In The Door

You've just graduated from a music or audio engineering school (or about to) and it's likely that you'll have technical and audio programming skills. Even so, the more skills you can offer a potential employer, the better, including the following:

- 10-key

- Accounting

- Collections

- Copyright law, especially international copyright law. You don't need to be a lawyer to understand the basics. In the creative industries, your salary depends on it!

- Knowledge of "Big Names" in the biz, especially in specific areas such as production, gaming, mixing, radio, retail, online and physical distribution, etc. Better yet . . . if you actually know some of these people.

- Knowledge of FCC licensing

- Knowledge of SoundScan and BDS, and how to read and interpret the data

- Music publishing—who gets paid and how?

- People skills including managing people, leading a team, getting things done, working with unusual or difficult personalities, diffusing tense situations, calming hysterical people

- Project management—starting something and finishing it, without excuses.

- Research

- Royalties

- Second language (more languages is even better). To go along with this, knowledge of cultural customs and practices in other countries is hugely helpful.

- Typing (at least 60 wpm)

How to Respond to Request for Fee or Salary Requirements

Some employers ask you to submit salary requirements with your résumé and cover letter, or will pin you down in an interview, or ask how much of a fee you'd like. Avoid revealing this information. Without inside knowledge, you could easily price yourself too high or too low, neither of which is favorable to you. Keep in mind that whoever mentions a number first loses.

You can't know what the job is worth until you know the employer's expectations and specific responsibilities for the position. When prompted to complete questions about "desired salary," consider writing, "prefer to discuss" or "negotiable." Also, consider this language for your cover letter:

"I acknowledge your request for a salary requirement. As you can see from my experience, I am more than qualified for XXX position, however, having never held a position specifically like this before, I would prefer to discuss the scope of the job with you before submitting my salary requirement. Besides, it's far more important to me to enjoy my job and co-workers. If this isn't the case, no salary could entice me to work at ZZZ Company."

If you are able to get any insider information through a friend or colleague already employed at the company to which you are applying, use this information to make your proposal. Also consider calling people in similar positions at similar companies. Don't overlook cold-calling. If you get someone on the phone during a cold call, be honest, ask what the salary range is for X, Y, or Z type positions. The value of research on this point cannot be emphasized enough. Failure to do your research could cost you literally thousands of dollars. Take the time to do it; you'll be glad you did.

Benefits in your salary history may add about 40% additional compensation. Therefore, consider writing a salary "range" on the application form incorporating your total compensation, calculating the salary you anticipate at your next performance evaluation, and add 15% for incentive negotiations.

Sometimes the money just isn't there. As noted previously, work on establishing relationships first and the money will follow. Nevertheless, in your opening negotiation, if the money isn't what you think it should be, explore some of the compensation alternatives listed below in lieu of salary. Having a company supply you with a cell phone, flexible work schedule or expense account is valuable, especially since these things are frequently easier for the company to "justify." Plus, these perks are mostly tax-free. Some of these alternatives what you might find available at a corporate job, many may also be available in the studio/production world. Just ask!

Compensation Alternatives

FINANCIAL

Bonus plan/revenue or profit sharing
Commission
Early compensation review
Expense account
Low-cost loan
Matching gifts
Moving expenses/relocation fees
Signing bonus
Spouse relocation assistance
Stock and stock options

BENEFITS

401K/retirement/pension plans
Accidental death insurance
Dental/optical insurance
Life insurance/supplemental life
Major medical insurance

EXTRAS

Annual physical
Club memberships/entertainment privileges
Company car/auto expense reimbursement
Company credit cards
Day care
Dependent scholarships
First-class travel
Gym
Legal advice
Memberships in professional associations
Pension
Personal use of frequent flyer miles
Professional certification/association fees
Publication incentives
Tax/financial/estate planning assistance
Training and education
Transportation allowance

Travel accident insurance
Upgraded air travel and hotels

SEVERANCE

Access to outplacement
Continuation of health insurance
Severance/employment agreement

TIME & LOCATION

Flex-time
Personal holidays
Telecommuting
Paid or unpaid sabbatical
Vacation
Severance pay

EQUIPMENT

Blackberry or other mobile device
Cellular phone
Computer
Pager

Your salary history is not relevant to the job you're applying for and employers may use the information as a gauge for current salary negotiations. In the interview, tell the employer you would be happy to discuss your salary history when it is determined that you are the best candidate for the job. You want an employer to imagine you in the position before discussing money. If pressed, ask the employer why your salary history is pertinent to the job opening. Decide whether to politely express that your salary history does not appear necessary to determine whether your qualifications are a good fit for the job, then get back to discussing the job responsibilities. A good strategy is to counter a question with another question, and ask, "What is the salary range for this position?"

CHAPTER 10

When You Get The Gig—Producer Fee Ranges and Considerations

The following is excerpted from a 2008 NARIP workshop featuring Dina LaPolt, Esq. and Zach Katz, Esq. who negotiated a producer agreement. These producer duties, deal points and fee ranges may help you in your next negotiation, and are provided courtesy of Dina LaPolt. These points favor the artist.

Producer's Duties

A producer's duties include producing, editing and sometimes mixing. When entering into an agreement, make sure to list all creative services in the agreement that Producer will perform.

EXAMPLE: "Producer will render 'all services' as a musician, arranger, conductor, programmer, etc. at recording sessions as and when requested by Artist." If this is not clearly specified, a Producer may come back and request more money.

In rap, R&B and pop, the producer usually co-writes the music. Be careful if an artist has a song that is already completed! The Copyright Act says a song is "melody and lyrics" but sometimes Producers try and get a piece of the copyright for just arranging a song. WATCH OUT!

Producer Advance (Old School)

The record company advances producer a "fee" on behalf of the Artist and then pays all recording costs. The advance will be determined largely on the success of producer's earlier recordings.

According to attorney and author Donald Passman:

"C" List/New Producers: $0 to $2,500/$3,500 per track ($25,000 to $35,000 per LP)

"B" List/Mid-Level: $3,500 to $7,500 per track ($35,000 to $75,000 per LP)

"A" List/Superstar: $10,000 plus (more like $50,000 plus per track)

"All-in" Producer Fund (Most Cases)

Digidesign's Pro Tools has revolutionized the way in which music is created. With the emergence of Pro Tools, most producers have their own recording studios. Producer gets an *All-In Fund*: Producer's fee *plus* recording costs. We are in a *producer-heavy* period.

"C" List: On "spec" or flat fee for a bunch of tracks (i.e., $5,000 for 6 songs)

"B" List: On "spec" or flat fee from $5,000 to $25,000 per track

"A" List: On "spec" or from $50,000 to $150,000 per track

Most "A" list producers do not produce tracks on "spec" or based on speculation of a song's future success.

Remixer: Creates all new music (or a "remix" of a song). Fee is usually very high because the remixer knows there are no points available (unless the original Producer agrees to a royalty *reduction* in the event artist brings in a remixer).

Producer Advance Versus Recording Costs

Usually one-third of the All-In Fund is deemed a "Producer's Fee" and the remaining two-thirds are deemed the "Recording Costs."

Example: $20,000 All-In Fund: $6,600 is the Producer's Fee and $13,400 is Recording Costs. The higher the Producer's Fee is in an All-In Fund situation, the better it is for the Artist.

Producer's Fee is recouped *first* at the Net Artist's Royalty Rate because Producer's Fee is clumped into Artist's "recording costs," *then* the Producer's Fee is *secondly* recouped from the Producer's Royalty Rate.

Trigger point in getting paid is further away which is *better* for the Artist.

The Producer Royalty

Try to keep the Producer Royalty to 3% pro-rated! Most producers will agree to 3%, because it is customary and standard in the industry.

Rule of Thumb: 1% pro-rated is equal to .01 (one penny)

"A" List	3% to 5%
"B" List	3%
"C" List:	3%

Producers are paid retroactive to Record One versus Prospectively, unlike the Artist!

Original Producer agrees to have his royalty reduced if Artist brings in a third party remixer.

Producer's royalty goes up by ½ point at gold and platinum sales. *Never agree to this unless the artist has escalations from record company!*

DISCLAIMER

Note: The information contained in the foregoing materials is provided solely for educational and general informative purposes and shall not be deemed legal advice.

11

Success Strategies— Some Parting Advice

Most of us share the desire to work hard and be recognized. Success, however, is rarely handed to us. We must create it ourselves. No one owes us a job. It's up to us to find paths of conduct that are ethical, satisfying and that encourage growth and opportunity in our work.

Perhaps the best advice to those who wish to advance themselves is to learn, baby, learn, and interact with an informed peer group. The key to career advancement is a commitment to lifetime education, to expanding your knowledge, vision and point of view. Every person is more valuable to his employer when he not only understands how things work, but why. Continuing education is an absolute necessity in maintaining your unique value.

The Nine Things Employers Wish You Knew

1. I'm not responsible for your career trajectory, I just need to get someone in here to do a job and don't want to have to worry about advancing a new hire's career. Please don't come onboard and expect to be instantly promoted. Don't wait for your career to be handed to you. Go out and get it! Take responsibility for your own career, take it into your own hands. Take your music and talents out into the world, create a market for them.

2. The way in which you approach your job search (which is a job in itself) is the way you'll approach any job I may offer you. Therefore if you're lazy and middle-of-the-road in your approach to getting my attention and an interview, if you're not enthusiastic and you don't believe in your own value, why should I hire you? Stand out a bit, be creative—in your cover letter, in how you reach me (via pizza delivery, Fed Ex or otherwise) or just with a good honest letter.

3. Follow directions! If I ask for a résumé as a Word doc attachment, that's what I mean!

4. Tell me something interesting about yourself. Just because a cover letter isn't required with a résumé doesn't mean you shouldn't send one. Let a glimmer of your personality come through but save the jokes for later. Let me know who you are and why I should hire you. Give me real reasons, and save the clichés and platitudes for someone else. Good writing goes far, and it doesn't have to be fancy.

5. Emphasize the benefits you'll bring me and my company if I hire you, don't tell me about mundane tasks you performed and fill your résumé with meaningless phrases. Show me evidence of your accomplishments, problems you solved and results you achieved.

6. Be prepared. Show that you know something about me and my company, ask intelligent questions that demonstrate you've (at least!) looked at the company's Website. Impress me with a few facts about my company, show me that you care, and that this isn't a drive-through interview.

7. Show me respect and manners, show up on time (if not early), dress appropriately for your interview, and be courteous to my staffers and subordinates. They matter.

8. It's not about YOU when you interview (or get the job), it's about ME (the employer), my company and challenges. It's about what needs to be done.

9. Don't bad-mouth your last company, boss or situation because I know that's how you might talk about me! Put the best positive spin you can on it and remain truthful.

Ten Things You Can Do Today

1. Introduce yourself to someone new
2. Call three people
3. Conduct a "gratitude visit" (see Martin Seligman's book on happiness in my list of suggested reading later)
4. Dedicate your work/job search to someone, whether it's a family member or someone who has always inspired you
5. Read a book
6. Power of now. Enjoy this moment, use it!
7. Write down your goals—personal and professional. Every day, do three things toward those goals.
8. Put your imagination to work on positive outcomes, rather than negative ones (worry). Imagine the best possible outcome to this situation. It's just as easy to think about the good as it is the bad.
9. Public speaking—just do it! Take a class, get over your fear of it, when you speak, you lead!
10. Take a risk, be daring. Your life is yours to live. Are you living it well? Or are you living someone else's idea of what your life should be?

Tess Taylor's Recommended Reading List: Books

When I hear people say they have no time to read, I laugh softly to myself. That's like saying you have no time to learn or improve. How ridiculous. Take a leaf from my father's book: he carries something to read with him wherever he goes, which I do too—you'll find a dozen opportunities every day to read a page or two if you have a book with you. It's a wonderful habit. If you think the cost of education (and the time it takes) is too high, consider the cost of ignorance. The key to continued success is having an edge and an education. Besides, a library card is free. All these books support the common goal of improving your plan, skills and effectiveness in life, understanding what works and what doesn't, and becoming the best possible version of yourself.

Happy reading!

☛ *A Whole New Brain* by Daniel Pink

☛ *Artist Development: A Distinctive Guide To the Music Industry's Lost Art* by Eugene Foley

☛ *Authentic Happiness* by Martin E.P. Seligman, Ph.D.

☛ *Benjamin Franklin's Secret of Success And What It Did For Me* by Frank Bettger

☛ *Buzz Marketing: Get People To Talk About Your Stuff* by Mark Hughes

☛ *Elements of Style* by Strunk & White

☛ *Grow Rich With Peace of Mind* by Napoleon Hill

☛ *How to Succeed in Business by Breaking All The Rules* by Dan S. Kennedy

☛ *How to Win Friends and Influence People* by Dale Carnegie

☛ *Indie Marketing Power* by Peter Spellman

☛ *Influence: The Psychology of Persuasion* by Dr. Robert B. Cialdini

☛ *Life is a Contact Sport* by Ken Kragen

☛ *Made To Stick: Why Some Ideas Survive & Others Die* by Chip Heath & Dan Heath

☛ *Making Money Make Music (An Insider's Guide to Becoming Your Own Music Publisher)* by Eric Beall

☛ *Man's Search for Meaning* by Viktor E. Frankl

☛ *Never Eat Alone* by Keith Ferrazi

☛ *No B.S. Time Management* by Dan Kennedy

☛ *Power Schmoozing* by Terri Mandell

- ☞ *Rich Dad, Poor Dad* by Robert Kiyosaki

- ☞ *Secrets of Power Persuasion* by Roger Dawson

- ☞ *Secrets of the Millionaire Mind* by T. Harv Eker

- ☞ *The 7 Habits of Highly Effective People* by Stephen Covey

- ☞ *The Four Agreements: A Practical Guide to Personal Freedom* by Don Miguel Ruiz

- ☞ *The New Psycho-Cybernetics: The Original Science of Self-Improvement and Success That Has Changed the Lives of 30 Million People* by Maxwell Maltz, M.D., F.I.C.S.

- ☞ *The Power of Now* by Eckhart Tolle

- ☞ *The Success Strategy* by Lester Korn

- ☞ *The Tightwad Gazette* by Amy Dacyczn

- ☞ *The Tipping Point* by Malcolm Gladwell

- ☞ *The War of Art* by Steven Pressfield

- ☞ *Think and Grow Rich* by Napoleon Hill

- ☞ *Write It Down, Make It Happen* by Henriette Anne Klauser

Your Favorites?

Got any favorite books? Drop me a line and let me know, especially ones that changed your life or that you found fascinating and couldn't put down. I would love your recommendations to expand my reading list! I read everything, fiction and non-fiction. E-mail me at tess@narip.com with "My Favorite Book(s)" in the subject line and it will get special attention. Check out NARIP's Bookshelf for future reading recommendations at www.narip.com.

Tess Taylor's Recommended Reading List: Blogs & News

☛ Bob Lefsetz, music industry news and blog: lefsetz.com

☛ Dan Kennedy, excellent advice for the feisty entrepreneur: dankennedy.com

☛ Digital Music News' Daily Snapshot, an good summary of developments in the music-tech space: digitalmusicnews .com

☛ HITS, music industry news: hits.com

☛ Michael Senoff's Hard to Find Seminars, excellent interviews and transcripts (all FREE) of fascinating and successful entrepreneurs from all walks of life. www .hardtofindseminars.com

☛ Penelope Trunk's Brazen Careerist blog, great career advice: penelopetrunk.com.

☛ Pho List, named after the Vietnamese soup ("pho"), this list addresses news and developments in the music-tech space, and marketing breakthroughs are frequently shared here: pholist.org

☛ Publicity Hound. Author and über-publicist Joan Stewart has excellent resources and knows how to generate attention. I love her weekly newsletter and have bought a number of her products. Publicityhound.com

Your Favorites?

Got any favorite blogs or news sources? Drop me a line and let me know! E-mail me at tess@narip.com with "My Favorite Blogs" in the subject line and it will get special attention.

The Rest Is Up to You

There will be obstacles in your career. But you knew that. The largest obstacle to your success will most likely be you. The good news is that's totally fixable with goals, risk-taking and discipline. Program yourself to succeed. Cast aside your fears, don't let them rule you—most of them are irrational anyway, and leap into the chaos where others fear to dip their toe. You'll find oceans of opportunity there.

Uncertainty is everywhere. And when nothing is certain, anything is possible.

Each one of you reading this has greatness in you. Let no one tell you otherwise.

I wish you the best of luck in your excellent career!

"If I believe I cannot do something, it makes me incapable of doing it. But when I believe I can, I acquire the ability to do it, even if I did not have the ability in the beginning."—Mahatma Gandhi, political and spiritual leader

Introduction: Adapting to a Changing World

By now, three things should be clear.

☞ The music business is in transition between older business models (major record labels) and newer ones (digital distribution, video games etc).

☞ Success in this business depends on your contacts—its who you know less than what you know.

☞ Success in this business requires dedication, perseverance and passion. There is no easy money here but with a lot of hard work, there can be a lot of money here.

Nowhere is this seen as a potential for growth as it is in the world of independent CD releases (or Internet digital-only releases as the case may be). In this world, Steffen Franz is an authority.

Steffen runs the Independent Distribution Collective—a company dedicated to distributing the CDs of independent artists. Steffen manages the distribution and sales of over 100 labels and each of their artists and albums. As quoted on his Website,

"Using the "Strength in Numbers" concept, and employing grassroots and industry-tested practices, IDC has created a whole new avenue for current and next generation artists who are trying to bring their music to the public."

For those of you who are looking to be in the music business as an artist, producer or both, this next section will be helpful for understanding how you (and your business, which really is you) should think about fitting into the market. Steffen lays out the territory of both the major labels and the independent labels for you and makes a great introduction to the world of business plans.

Why do you need a business plan? Because whether you believe it or not, YOU are your own business! Artists and Producers (more and more the same, these days) are not just the talent—they are the enterprise doing business. If this is the life you want, you need to understand that you are the business and there's no better way to begin to start your business than by creating a business plan.

While this is not a subject matter commonly discussed among artists and producers, it is increasingly important that you recognize and get comfortable with the functions of business and entrepreneurship. The business plan will help you get smart and organized about how to successfully get your artist/business off the ground.

It is crowded out there and getting more so everyday. Are you sure that you're the person that your prospective client wants to work with? Great!

Now how do you convince them of that???

—Matt Donner

12

How Am I Really Going to Make Money in This Business?

Success in the music business is about promoting and marketing yourself and most independent artists have to be entrepreneurial in that they must do this themselves before any label or management entity will work with them. Ultimately every artist must honestly answer the question, "How am I going to make money doing this?"

The desire to be your own successful boss has always been at the heart of the music business, but this success requires self-motivation, passion and determination. The secret to success in the Music Business is having a combination of strong will, talent, good organizational skills, and a basic understanding of business. To take your music from a basement or home studio into a professional business also requires patience, as growth typically comes gradually.

For many, the appeal of the music business is only partly the music itself. We are drawn to music's emotional power over us and are also attracted by the freedom associated with the business of music. Many of us are not cut out for the traditional 9 to 5 grind, or we may not do well professionally in a subordinate role—we think we're better bosses than employees! The life of a musician almost always involves a certain freedom of time and creative expression. As such, we all want to be our own bosses, which is the essential element of entrepreneurship.

To this end, many desire to have this freedom but don't have the diligence to make it happen. Many would-be artists or musicians become employees as a result. It is far riskier to "roll your own" than to simply take a paycheck. How many "weekend warriors" do you know in the music business? Worse, how many people work in unrelated businesses to earn financial security, only to dream of working in this business? In the end, working in the music industry requires a sort of "gusto"—whether or not you open your own business. Truth is, there are just as many entrepreneurs as there are employees in our business!

There are several paths to becoming an entrepreneur, many fraught with pitfalls or sure-fire disasters. Many start by breaking the piggy bank, or borrowing a parent's credit card to go buy gear. This could be your first guitar, your first synthesizer, or a collection of gear that the guy at the music store told you that you *must* have to become a successful producer. Several thousand dollars later, you may be sitting on a paperweight collection with no idea of how to set it all up, connect it all—much less make music with it. There are support options out there, from hiring the guy who sold you the stuff in the first place to paying for online support or watching countless hours of free videos on the Internet. While many of these options are "free," they may cost you dearly in terms of time and frustration. You will likely have to wade through weeks of material to piece together answers to your initial questions. This can be a colossal waste of time and money, and still, unfortunately, it happens every day.

Another way to start a business is to procure an outside funding source such as a personal or commercial loan. Unfortunately, qualifying for a loan is harder than just filling out an application. Banks don't just give money out—regardless of the interest rate. You need a plan that goes much deeper than "If I buy the gear, I'll be a producer and someday, I'll be rich and famous."

Nice dream. It just doesn't work that way.

To avoid the bank scrutiny and interest rates, many borrow from the "International Bank of Grandma"—relying on the faith and love of family to fund the dream. This can be equally unrealistic because the initial question still hasn't been answered– just how the hell are you going to make money doing this? Running a business means qualifying every decision you make and every dollar you spend. You're not going to get rich charging people $20/hour to make records that are given away at shows in the hopes that they'll come see your band again.

Not anymore.

COACH'S CORNER: Making the Right Steps Forward

So how do you make money in the music business? As mentioned earlier, you need to be dedicated, talented, passionate, and well trained. Talent and passion may have been instilled at birth, but dedication and education can be learned and earned. Reading this book is one of many steps towards your success and understanding that learning is a life-long endeavor will keep you sharp.

To be a successful entrepreneur, you must first learn the business. The concept of apprenticing, interning or mentoring is an age-old and yet completely valid process. While some people are born with talent and money (read: lucky), most people (the other 95%) need training. This training can take the shape of a traditional scholastic education and/or a mentorship. It can also be as an employee for another company, learning the business on their watch.

Often, building your business means a few years of hard work for someone else learning the ropes, all the while banking a portion (10% or 20%) of your income as a start-up fund for your own business. After these formative years, you should understand how money flows into and out of the business and you can hopefully start your business without the financial stress of a loan. This lowers your monthly overhead, making you more likely to be successful from dollar one.

Keep in mind that most new businesses fail within the first three years due to either lack of appropriate funds, inexperience or simple mismanagement. Training under a qualified mentor can help you avoid these common mistakes.

This apprenticeship mentality allows for up-and-coming entrepreneurs to experience failure and learn from their mistakes. But be careful—too many mistakes on your employers' dime will cost you your job! Apprenticing is reminiscent of a time when one would have to apprentice before being given a shot to run things on their own.

Many people attempt to run a business right out of the gate with no prior experience. They feel that learning from someone else will stymie their creativity and teach them someone else's style—not help them develop their own (musicians are famous for thinking they can figure it out on their own without any coaching or training!) The biggest pitfall of this approach is that regardless of how well-capitalized the start-up business is, or how well-connected an entrepreneur is to the core of his or her business, without any real life experience it is very hard to anticipate the ups and downs of the business and thereby be successful. Early mistakes can drown the business in debt or worse—completely miss the customer base. *Thinking* you have the right business plan for the right market and *proving* it are entirely different things.

Before anyone can make the decision to become an entrepreneur, it is important to decide what role to play in business. Do you become an employee in a business related to your career goals, or do you take an unrelated day job based on the income you can earn? Do you work for a year for someone else, for a much smaller salary with the hope of learning enough to run your own business in the near future? Or should you muster the guts to go-it-alone after obtaining a bank loan?

These questions must be answered before entering the job market. If you have already chosen your path before you are expected to perform professionally, then the direction of your training will be clearer and will more likely point you towards your end goal. The first question one must ask is "Am I an employee or am I an entrepreneur?"

Employee Versus Entrepreneur: Which Is Right for You?

To clearly understand which title fits your personality, you must determine which of these roles best defines you.

An employee is someone who works for another person for a wage or salary. An entrepreneur is defined as someone who organizes, manages, and assumes the risks of a business or enterprise. Clearly these are two very different paths as entrepreneurship includes a far greater amount of risk than being an employee. It is this assumption of risk that definitively separates these roles.

COACH'S CORNER: Tasking for Cash

Most of us have been an employee at one point or another in our lives as far back as our childhood. Any child who has been given an allowance by their parents in trade for some chore like mowing the lawn is an employee in the simplest of terms. Parents expect things like your room to be clean or the trash being taken out in exchange for this salary. They are assuming the risk of running the home—from covering room and board, education through the high school (and hopefully college level) as well as other basic living expenses. It becomes more like a job (and you more like an employee) when there are specific tasks that are expected in trade for money.

In today's job market, finding work is easiest when you know someone—or really that someone knows you. You still have to be qualified, but if you have a family friend running a business close to your desired career path, it makes perfect sense to spend a year or two working for this person, earning money and valuable experience towards starting your own business. It's a big help when you know someone in the biz! But is that enough to start your own?

Risk/Reward Ratios and Determining a Pathway for Your Career

It is difficult to determine a pay scale for someone who creates or records music. There is no real scale to price creative services in the industry and sometimes, younger *is* better. The range of skills needed to be a producer in today's industry is wide—from simple beat making to mixing and promotions, there's a lot to learn, so the sooner you get started, the better.

How many years will it take to reach a level of experience that allows you to produce your own works professionally? One year? Three? Five? More? It is impossible to put a timeline on how long it might take a given individual to develop these skills into a service that can garner a fair wage. After having spent years becoming a great composer, engineer or producer, it won't do you much good if you don't have any experience selling those skills or services. This is a critical error in many careers: the inability to seal a deal and/or deliver on your client's expectations.

Before investing time and money into your training, you should know the "real-world" value of the investment in those skills and the risk-to-reward ratio. In other words, what do I have to risk to become successful, and what type of reward might I get in return for these skills or services? If I invest $100,000 to get a degree in French literature, does that allow me

COACH'S CORNER: Overcoming Obstacles

Whether they realize it or not, people start making decisions about their future at an early age. The sooner someone starts learning something, the sooner they'll be proficient at their chosen skill. However, being good but young could communicate inexperience to a customer. As a businessperson and/or entrepreneur, you must overcome these concerns by demonstrating your professionalism and skill, providing professional references, or even discounting the rate on their initial project with you, which gives you the opportunity to prove your value to them.

to have a career as a college professor making $35,000 per year? Will that pay my rent and bills and allow me to save for the future while potentially having to pay back that initial $100,000 investment plus interest? Do I pay $30,000 to learn how to compose and mix music that can make me thousands for just one of my compositions—or leave me broke if I sell none?

Once you've figured out what you enjoy doing and how much it will cost to become skilled enough to do it for a successful career, the next step is to figure out what type of market there is for your proposed service. This will help you to determine if this career choice is viable.

Can't Beat 'Em?

It may be that your competition profile is all much further along than you. How can you compete with even the smallest player in this case? Maybe you can't. Well if you can't beat 'em, join 'em.

In studying your future competition, you've also compiled a list of would-be employers! Now, you can target this list and submit your résumé from which will ideally come an interview. At this point, I highly suggest you return to Section 2 and reread Tess' work on résumés. When the offer has been made to you, come back to this section.

Once you've obtained a position, use these next few years of employment to understand how their business operates (while at the same time putting some money in your pocket). The associations and connections you make as an employee could prove vital to *your* future business.

Most people will start their career in the role of employee. Being an employee allows aspiring entrepreneurs to learn the business first-hand, make valuable industry contacts, and raise (read: save) much-needed start-up capital. This path is less risky than just getting and spending money on your unproven idea.

Assuming that this works for you (even for a short while), you may be ready to start your own business—or are you? Ask yourself, "Am I ready to take this step? Do I have enough money, and a living situation that will allow me to move onto this next level?" No business starts with zero capital and you should be prepared by having money in the bank to keep you fed, housed and clothed for at least six months to a year. Are you *sure* you're ready?

13

How the Music Business Works

Roles in the Music Business

There are no shortages of places in the music industry to find work or open a business. This industry has so many business types that it can be hard to determine where you see yourself working—both as an employee and as a business owner. The following few sections are designed to give you an overview of many of those areas within the industry.

You'll see here and in the section afterwards ("Overview of the Music Business") that much of the industry stems from the need to sell records, which, at its heart, comes from record labels. They are the ones taking the record out of the studio and into the market. No matter what you think you know about record labels, they are one of the most important businesses within this industry.

Keep in mind that these are very much oriented towards the "business" of music, not the production of music.

Record Labels

There are two types of record labels: the major record labels and the independent record labels. The biggest difference between them is simple: Money. They both use the same basic business model (which is to produce, own and sell music), and both have distribution channels for marketing and promotion.

The Majors: In the early days of records and record labels, the workflow was to pair artists with songwriters and arrangers, performers and then recording studios to produce the recording. Major labels (ones that were good at artist development and sales) would often invest significant capital to build cutting-edge recording studios that would be used by all of the artists and producers associated with the label. A&M studios and Sony studios are good examples—the label owns the studio that it hires to produce the records for itself! These studios would later open to the public, but in the early years were reserved for the label and their artists.

In addition to the purchase and construction of recording facilities, the major labels also heavily invested in manufacturing. By also owning the manufacturing facilities that produce the physical product (first vinyl LPs and then later cassette tapes and ultimately CDs), the majors were able to "eliminate the middleman" by also controlling the means of production, and thereby maximize profit. The majors now control some of the largest music manufacturing companies in the world and create about 80% of the retail consumer Compact Discs available today. There are only about 100 large-scale *independent* CD manufacturers in the world today.

Another area where labels continue to be involved is in the promotion of a new or established artist. Major labels are able to create demand and hype for their artists and bands without ever hiring someone from the outside. The underlying agenda in all of this is simple: sales. For the past 25 years the majors have owned and operated their own distribution companies, which maximizes their profit. The sale of physical units (CDs etc.) is still one of the most lucrative revenue streams for these companies so it makes sense that they created and developed their own companies to focus on selling their product to retailers.

Historically, major labels have been able to take an artist who lives in some obscure town and make them into a superstar in (what seems like) an overnight success. A great example of this is an 18-year-old Beck, who made his first recordings on a 4-track in his bedroom. Within a few short months of being discovered he was in a studio with the "Dust Brothers" making his debut album.

For many, this is the "holy grail" of the business—to be an overnight sensation.

However, it's really a needle in the haystack business model for an artist and one that is begging for disappointment—it just doesn't happen that often and the odds are stacked against it happening to *you*.

It should be emphasized that all of the "stardom" that may come from signing with a major label comes at a price. An unproven artist signing to a major label will generally retain less than 10% of the total profits from their album—10%! This is after all of the upfront expenses (studio time, producer's fees, manufacturing costs, marketing and promotions, tour support etc.) are paid back. Many major label artists cannot pay back the advance on the first or even second record! So when *do* they get paid?

CD sales are down—way down—and major labels are getting hard-pressed to find profit in any aspect of an artist career that it can. To that end, many are now taking shares of merchandise sales and touring revenues, called an "Artist360" deal. These deals extend well beyond the traditional splits of sales and publishing shares to splitting touring revenue, merchandise profits and virtually every other source of income derived by the artist (many of which were considered off limits as recently as five years ago). They literally own the artist's work—360 degrees of it.

Independents: Typically an independent label will advance much less money than a major, and may not even cover the cost of making the record itself. The artist or band may pay out of pocket for all of the recording costs and then the label takes responsibility for manufacturing, marketing, and promotion. This means that the label and the artist can recoup their expenses more quickly and then divide any profit in a much more "artist-friendly" manner.

It should also be noted that in the past decade, there have been many single artist labels popping up. This model places all of the risk on the artist and allows/forces them to personally pay out all upfront expenses, but having to share none of the profit. A good example of this is the band Fugazi, who owns the label, the studio, and the touring company, and sell their own show tickets as well. They've eliminated the need for a major label completely.

Figure 11 shows market share sales (domestic on left; worldwide on right) that compares the "Big Four" majors versus independents (fiscal year ending 2005). The U.S. music market shares are according to Nielsen SoundScan (2005); the world market figures are according to IFPI (2005). Nielsen SoundScan reported that the Big Four record labels accounted for 81.87% of the entire US music market in 2005.

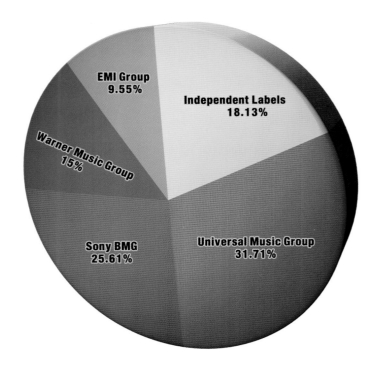

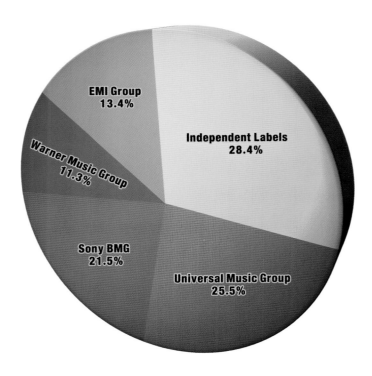

Figure 11: *Graphical representations of the Majors versus Independents, Domestic (top) versus International (bottom).*

Distributor

The goal of a distribution company is to help a record label place an artist's music in stores (or online stores) and act as a middleman between the label and retail stores and Websites. Distributors have little other responsibility, other than to warehouse product and cultivate relationships with major store chains and thousands of independent stores across the country.

The first distributors of music-related products were small independent companies whose representatives traveled to various regions to sell their product. This changed in the 1950s and 1960s as the bigger record labels decided to control their relationships with retail stores and chains. In those days it was all about winning support of retailers and these major label-owned distributors had the muscle to get a new artist in the door of any major store or chain.

Things changed in the 1970s for independent artists and labels as some of the first independent distribution companies were born. In 1970 there were only two niche distribution companies (primarily centered around jazz and blues artists) But by the late '70s, there were dozens of these distributors.

Over the next 20 years, the independent distribution company flourished, demonstrated by the establishment of hundreds of small distribution companies. Some of them became so successful that the majors had to seek out and acquire them, which has resulted in a few large companies owning most of the "independent" companies. Today, there are still the "Big Four" major label distribution companies, plus four or five major independent distribution companies (owned in part or in full by the majors). This does not include digital distribution, in which the majors have been ramping up investment since 2000.

There is a large difference in the money to be earned by the distributor between majors and independents. A typical fee paid by a major label to its distribution arm could be anywhere from a few cents to a few dollars per unit. The basic fee charged to independent labels ranges from a fixed dollar or dollar-fifty per unit for a full-length album to about 30% of all wholesale sales. This would most likely apply for artists or labels who have "P and D" (also known as a Production/Manufacturing and Distribution deal) deals in which the distributor actually covers the upfront costs of manufacturing.

COACH'S CORNER: Changing Means of Distribution

Look for distribution models to change, as the increase in online sales presents great opportunities for independents to sell their music. With the growth of companies like CD Baby for online fulfillment or Amazon.com (who are buying more and more product from independents), the ability for a small label or even a single artist to sell in stores all across the country is rapidly increasing, potentially eliminating the need for a distributor. Digital distribution and many other "new media" distribution models will be discussed in depth a little further on into this book.

Manager

A manager is someone who partners with an artist or band to negotiate with the record label, booking agents, licensing entities, and/or provide general career and legal advice. The manager has traditionally been the voice of the artist (in terms of negotiation with anyone who wanted to use or sell the artist's published works). The manager is often responsible for getting the artist or band into the studio, creating an image for them, and matching them with a team of promotional staff who can help get the word out about the group or artist. Managers are also conduits to investors who can help raise much needed capital to fund the marketing plan. In some cases this is covered by a record deal, but in many cases the label does not underwrite all of the costs involved with developing an artist or band. In many cases the manager might invest the money needed to help establish the band or artist. It is funding and connections that make the manager a valuable and viable member of the team.

A talented manager keeps his or her clients on track and organized, but also focuses on whatever goals the artist or band sets. In some ways the manager is an employee of the artist or band, whose goal is to make the band as successful as possible. An example of a great manager/artist relationship is that of Elvis Presley and Colonel Tom Parker. Parker's management of Elvis re-wrote the role of the manager and was seen as central to the astonishing success of Elvis' career. Even though Parker was dedicated entirely to his clients' interests, he took far more than the traditional 10% of Elvis's earnings (reaching 25% and up to 50% by the end of Elvis's life).

Booking Agent

The booking agent's main job is to negotiate performance engagements with venues and clubs. A booking agent's job is difficult, time intensive, and is often "feast or famine." In order for the agent to be successful, they must rely on their standing relationships within the industry. Even publicists and radio promoters communicate with the booking agent, who will alert them to bookings in areas where the band is getting press or radio play. Other duties of the booking agent include mapping out a tour of various regions and working with both the manager and the record label to support retail sales.

Another important role of the booking agent is to enforce an artist's contract and rider. Most bands don't have the muscle to deal with an uncooperative promoter—a good agent can retaliate against a delinquent promoter by "putting the word out" about someone who rips off their bands or breaches contract in any way.

Finally, a booking agent helps by pairing up the band with other artists on tour that might appeal to the same audience. This is a great way for up-and-coming artists to gain popularity. This allows the agent to grow the fan base of the lesser-known group. A booking agent generally gets paid 10% of all performance revenue from both the band's guarantee and any bonus money.

Other Possible "Team" Members

Publicist

A publicist is a public relations specialist who can write a press release and artist biography and has the contacts to disseminate stories and information about the artist or new releases to as many sources as possible. This dissemination is done by mail, e-mail, on various Websites and through various services that specialize in press release promotion. Publicists are used for all different types of marketing and promotional campaigns including professional athletes and teams, politicians, and traditional businesses—even musical instrument and audio gear manufacturers.

Promoters

Web Promoter: A web promoter is the Internet counterpart to the traditional publicist. Web Promoters use social and music networking Websites to get news about their clients' releases and tours to the public. They also help build an artist or band's fan base by communicating with the fans directly—a more personalized touch than a traditional publicist. They also help drive traffic to online sales points to help drive digital download sales. A typical web promoter could charge between a few hundred and a few thousand dollars per campaign, depending on the scope and duration of the work involved. Most promoters work from home on a consultation/contractor basis and focus on both the design of the WebPages and of course social networking as well.

Radio Promoter: A radio promoter has been at the heart of any big album or single release (or really any type of music industry promotion) for the past 40 or 50 years. These professionals market music to both terrestrial and digital radio stations with the hope of their clients entering the charts (and depending on the success of the artist or band) and creating overall demand on college, community and later commercial radio stations.

The role of the radio promoter has also seen a shift in the past few years, with many of them expanding to offer digital delivery of MP3s to program directors (in addition to the standard mailing of physical CDs). Most radio promoters work with a label before a CD is released to identify a single or two and determine how to best market the songs. This can make for a very effective campaign and costs anywhere from a few thousand dollars for an independent artist campaign, to a few hundred thousand dollars to target commercial radio with a mainstream single release.

CHAPTER 14

An Overview of the Traditional "Record" and the Wider Known "Music" Industry

The History

The traditional recording industry (or music industry as we now know it) began in the 1940s, although since the 1940s, there have been huge developments in the way people create, listen to, and purchase music. Nearly the only constant in the music industry is change—what was hip or "sellable" last year may not be trendy this year. The mega pop star that was tearing up the charts five years ago may have dropped entirely out of sight.

The early days of the music industry was made up of multiple strong independent labels. Initially, these labels were grown from the heartland of the United States in places like

COACH'S CORNER: Small Versus Major Labels

Many people think it is easy to record a song or an album at home in a bedroom studio and tomorrow it will be the number one album in the nation. Although this could happen (people do win the lottery, after all . . .), it is far more realistic to think that you might create something that will engage a small group of people on the local level. Many independent artists and smaller labels can't achieve chart-topping success on their own as they are either poorly organized, under-funded, or both.

This disorganization and lack of funding marks a sharp contrast to the major labels, who are organized and well funded. With 50 years of success under their belts, the majors have defined, refined and developed the music business into a well-oiled machine, churning out hit after hit, star after star. What the public doesn't see is the fact that for every star, there are thousands of artists, bands and start-up labels that fail—they're just not profitable enough for the majors to continue supporting.

Detroit, Memphis, and New Orleans and they spent their money exclusively on developing artists and touring. When the industry changed from every home having a radio, to every home having a record player, the industry changed from a business driven by songs and fans, to a business driven by product sales.

This was the beginning of the end for the early industry and although many people have great songs, it would ultimately become the majors who decided which would become hits—entirely based on potential sales, not musicality or artistry. Many of these independents later joined forces to become the four major labels we know today (EMI Group, Warner Music Group. Sony/BMG and the Universal Music Group). These four major labels are only responsible for 5% to 10% of the music released worldwide, but make up the vast majority of the total revenue in a $10 billion annual industry.

COACH'S CORNER: The Next Big Thing?

In the early days of the music industry, people wanted to find "the next big thing." They would search for a song they heard on the radio, and would drive to the local store, or call the radio station, just to find out who that new singer or song they heard was. This wave continued for close to 30 years. Between 1950 and 1980 the traditional record business was a growth industry, raking in profits greater and greater than the year before. There were more and more opportunities for artists as well, but they all stemmed from the idea that the more popular a band or singer became, the more profitable they would be for the record companies.

By 1980 the industry could see a revolution on the horizon as people continued to buy cassettes, LP albums and 45s (and even 8-tracks!) but the heyday of vinyl was seeing its twilight. The compact disc was initially developed to store music, but later expanded to other types of data storage. CDs have been commercially available since October, 1982. In 2009, they are still the standard physical medium for commercial audio recordings.

The industry saw huge growth again between 1985 (when Dire Straits "Brothers in Arms" was the first to sell 1 million CDs), and 2000 (when the Beatles "1" release saw 30 million CDs sold). This was the zenith of the record business, as the industry over these 15 years (1985–2000) had learned to maximize its profitability and could be counted on for constant growth year to year. The beginning of the end of the industry as we knew it was also on the horizon, with the inception and acceptance of the MP3 and digital music right around the corner. As of 2009, the music industry continued to lose steam in physical product sales, down close to 35% since 2000.

The State of the Union

Today there are thousands of albums released weekly in the United States, and thousands more across the world. Although there has been a decline in retail sales through every sector of the industry, the rise of the independent artist and record label, and the use of do-it-yourself or "DIY" marketing and promotion tactics and techniques have given the independents an edge early in the 21st century. Sales for major label artists continue to fall at an unprecedented rate, while small independents are posting gains year in and year out!

Many factors played a part in the fundamental profitability shift from bigger, well-developed artists to independent "break-through" artists. A milestone for this trend started in the early 1990s with the Seattle "grunge" scene, when small no-name artists and labels began racking up chart hits and hundreds of thousands in sales of their own. Within a year, many of the "indie" labels these artists signed with had been bought by one of the majors. In hindsight, this strategy was poorly executed as the majors acquired dozens of small labels, many of which could not be successful at the level the bigger companies needed to maintain their profitability.

The majors had become just another part of the rising trend of multi-national corporations investing in companies and then gutting them from the inside out to make them as profitable as possible. These corporations also own television stations and film production companies, which allowed them to cross-market their products and capitalize on the demand that any one division was seeing.

This strategy of buying established companies continues today in all genres and styles of music. A good independent can work for five to 10 years to establish its fan base and audience for their music. With a track record of success, it could then make a deal with a major company to get its music into retail outlets and placed in radio, TV and film. This all comes at a price, and if not done wisely, ends up being less profitable than the independent could have been on their own.

By the mid 1990s, one thing on the agenda for majors and independents alike was downsizing. Downsizing typically entails purchasing a smaller company, identifying any overspending, and cutting any aspects of the business that were not profitable. The first department that often saw cuts as a result of this "cost-effective" strategy was the A&R division (Artist and Repertory), whose main responsibility was finding and developing talent. Long gone were the days when a band could play a show and some "suit" in the background would come up afterwards and offer to make them stars.

COACH'S CORNER: The Turning Point

There is no more budget for major labels to actually scout and develop talent. They now rely on sales data and word of mouth hype to find new and emerging talent. This system is prone to failure, as there's no farm league for developing new talent. New pop stars do emerge, but most of the artists major labels are signing today are already a known entity.

The lack of artist development by the majors will eventually lead to a turning point in which the independent labels will not only be the trendsetters (as they have been in past years), but there is a high probability that they will actually become more profitable than the majors. This is possible because independents are able to retain all of the publishing and distribution rights and thereby give their artists a much more favorable split of the profits.

The only real certainty about the future of the music business is that it will constantly evolve. It will likely become more independent-friendly, with less importance placed on major label success. Regardless, to be competitive in this industry you must study the current business in detail, and understand where the major labels of the past failed. Also, study the trends in social networking, and use grassroots methods that have been tested over years. Formulate a company and a marketing plan that can succeed and grow in the *next* incarnation of the "record" business.

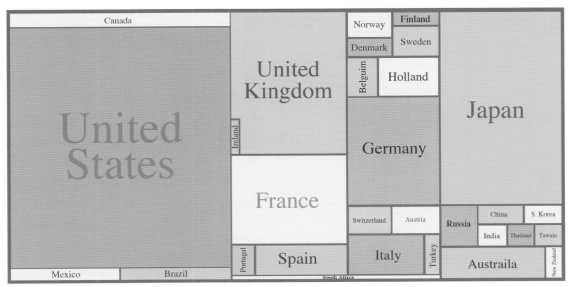

Figure 12: *A graphical representation of the size of various international music markets as of 2008. The larger sections represent the bigger markets. Drawn by Steve Hawtin based on widely quoted data from IFPI. Licensed under the GFDL by the author; Released under the GNU Free Documentation License.*

Rank	Country	Album Sales 2008	World Market Value 2008
1	USA	37-40%	30-35%
2	Japan	9-12%	16-19%
3	UK	7-9%	6.4-9.1%
4	Germany	7-8%	6.4-5.3%
5	France	4.5-5.5%	5.4-6.3%
6	Canada	2.6-3.3%	1.9-2.8%
7	Australia	1.5-1.8%	1.5-2.0%
8	Brazil	2.0-3.8%	1.1-3.1%
9	Italy	1.7-2.0%	1.5-2.0%
10	Spain	1.7-2.3%	1.4-1.8%
11	Netherlands	1.2-1.8%	1.3-1.8%
12	Mexico	2.1-4.6%	0.8-1.8%
13	Belgium	0.7-0.8%	0.8-1.2%
14	Switzerland	0.75-0.9%	0.8-1.1%
15	Austria	0.5-0.7%	0.8-1.0%
17	Russia	2.0-2.9%	0.5-1.4%
18	Taiwan	0.9-1.6%	0.5-1.1%
19	Argentina	0.5-0.7%	0.5-1.0%
20	Denmark	0.45-0.65%	0.5-0.8%

Figure 13: *Worldwide album sales and market value.*

Figure 12 shows the percentage of album sales and market value throughout the world in the late 1990s through the early 2000s. **Figure 13** shows the same International markets by sales as of 2008.

The "Wild West"

The current state of the music industry may best be described as the "Wild West" era of the business. The advances seen in file sharing, personal computing, and home recording, and the subsequent re-emergence of the independent label as a legitimate alternative to the majors has created new frontiers and opportunities for those on the forefront of the movement. In some ways, it is not unlike the 1950s, which were a pivotal and formative time, witnessing the birth of the original major labels. In 2009, it has never been easier to set up shop on the Internet and grow your career or a record label little by little until you are an established and profitable entity.

DVD: Studio-Side Chat
"Wild West"
Discussion of hits/
knowing your end user:
4:31–7:27

In the mid-1990s, the landscape for independent artists and labels changed forever with the explosive growth of the Internet. The ease with which a small group of people could now create digital promotional campaign and share information over the Internet was a first step toward leveling the playing field between the major labels and the independents. Previously, an up-and-coming artist or band could spend months on the road collecting mailing list information (actual physical addresses of fans) and send postcards or letters to let their fans know about upcoming shows and releases. Widespread acceptance of the personal computer and Internet changed all this. Bands and artists are now able to connect with these fans via e-mail and Websites, thereby increasing the circle of people without regard to where they were living (while simultaneously cutting the time and labor involved in getting the word out).

Another tipping point for the music industry of old was the inception of CD Baby and the rapid growth of web-based retailers like Amazon and eBay. These sites enabled independent artists to market products globally for the first time. This meant that now no one company (or Four) could control or limit the success of a developing artist, who could now sell directly to his/her end-users.

By early 2000, there were Websites like Napster and Kazaa, both of which hurt the major labels' revenue through widespread illegal P2P (peer-to-peer) file sharing. Although illegal, this new technology gave the independents the exposure and visibility that they needed to be successful. Almost overnight, fans could find music by groups and artists who were obscure only months or weeks before.

These early file-sharing Websites eventually gave rise to iTunes and other similar paid online music retailers. Apple's iTunes has become the leading music retailer in the world. These new digital file-sharing technologies, along with the huge growth of social networking (including the development and launch of MySpace and Facebook), have allowed independent artists and labels to reach more people than ever before. Where artists and labels used to spend hundreds if not thousands of dollars to design and develop their own Websites, these sites have allowed even the most unknown band to gain visibility and notoriety without spending dollar one on promotion.

Another pivotal development was the rise of YouTube, which is now the online video host for more than a billion videos. YouTube has allowed independents to produce and release music videos without having to buy their exposure from MTV or VH1. YouTube has enabled a new generation to post their music and videos for free, getting the word out to their fans through myriad newly developed social networking platforms.

Manufacturing

There are two key components of manufacturing as it relates to the music industry: the manufacturing of physical goods, and the distribution of those goods. Historically this distribution of goods was to physical (store-front) retailers, but has now evolved to include distribution directly to consumers through the Internet. Over time, most industries are able to minimize the cost of producing their product(s), but the music industry has turned this into an art form. The average cost of producing a single CD to the average independent artist or label is around $1.00 per unit. The major labels can mass-produce CDs at a rate as low as 29 cents per unit (a little higher for a double disc or DVD product). There are at least 100 reputable CD manufacturers in the USA, but none of them can manufacture product as cheaply as the major labels do for themselves. This extremely low manufacturing cost enables the majors to use the profits generated by CD sales for other costs such as the production of the music itself, as well as the associated marketing and promotion costs.

Cost of Goods Per Unit: Major Versus Independent Labels

In the 21st century, independent artists and labels can better compete as they have a much smaller overhead than their major label counterparts. The profit an independent can make could be close to the same per unit margin, on a much smaller scale. **Figure 14** details the difference between the retail prices of an independent and major label product and the costs involved.

Major Label

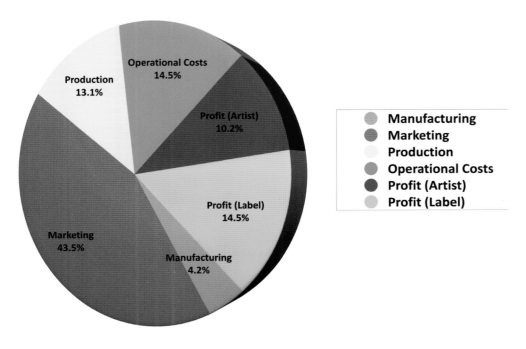

Independent Label

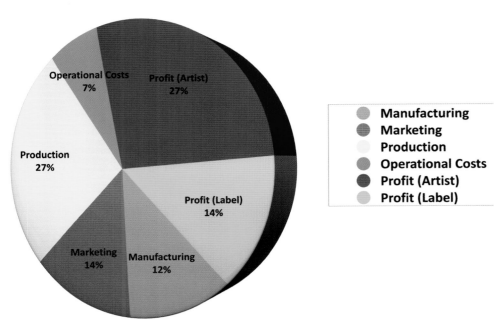

Figure 14: *The breakdown of costs per unit between major labels (top) and independents (bottom).*

DVD: Studio-Side Chat
Discussion of the CD/media
distribution: 9:30–12:22

Physical Product:

Until there is another type of media that becomes as widely accepted as the CD in major music retail markets, CDs will continue to be the primary physical product produced by the music industry.

In this age of the Internet and file sharing, one might ask, why physical products at all? The fact is, many average consumers want a tangible physical product. The majority of people that purchase music want to own the audio, the cover, the liner notes, the album credits, etc. In the 21st century, major and independent labels alike need to focus on those aspects of physical product that give even more added value to the consumer to continue to bolster physical sales.

The added value of physical product is the packaging and as of this writing, the *quality* of the audio itself. Though the compression algorithms used to create the smaller, compressed audio files (those file types that are available for download) are constantly improving, the fact remains that MP3, AAC and other common compressed file types have a lesser quality than their CD counterparts. Additionally, most labels are now looking to create distinctive packaging in place of the standard two-sided, uninformative packaging that once dominated the racks. These days, we're seeing more and more elaborate booklets and inserts to entice the consumer back to the physical product.

Another consumer enticement that's becoming increasingly common is "extra" or "bonus" content. Many labels are now releasing either double CD or CD/DVD packages with content that is unavailable through iTunes or other common file-sharing applications. The release of box sets are also often profitable for the labels as they long ago invested the production costs of producing the album(s), and now need only invest in new packaging and promotion. By putting together a nice presentation of these products, with the added bonus of some cool "extras," the labels have found a way to re-purpose an old product with very little overhead and thereby an excellent profit margin. Often these box sets and re-releases are billed as "collector's items" that are only available in limited quantity to create a sense of exclusivity and urgency to the consumer. While a CD's average Cost Of Goods Sold (COGS) is around $1 per average full length CD release (independents), these products might be more in the range of $10/unit COGS. This higher cost is offset by the fact that the average box set or "collector's pack" retails between $40 and $100.

Another major development in the world of physical manufacturing in the 21st Century has been a resurgence of vinyl. As a backlash against the "digitalization" of music in the late 1990s and early 2000s, the demand for vinyl has grown exponentially. This is a much-needed shot in the arm for physical music retailers. The upsurge of new and interesting physical product will help these retailers grow their business, and allow for a new era of physical releases. However, the next decade will likely see further decline in physical product sales as the speed of data transfer and the shrinking cost of storage will create more and more digital consumers. As a result, the world will eventually transition away from physical product within the next 15 or 20 years, with the physical products becoming the specialty market (CDs, vinyl, and box sets), that account for the same percent of total sales that digital sales do now.

Retail

The current music industry's core business model continues to be retail sales of its physical product (CDs, vinyl LPs, 12-inch and 7-inch singles, CD-Es, and CD/DVDs) through every distribution channel possible. These sales make up roughly 70% of all music sales in the United States. Outside of this core model, other revenue streams now include digital music sales, music licensing for film, TV and video games, and merchandising of brand related non-audio products (from t-shirts to water bottles to bumper stickers). Although the sales of digital music have seen growth over the past decade, it still remains at between 10 and 15 percent (depending on what data you believe) of overall annual U.S. music sales.

One of the most trusted sources for entertainment industry information is Nielsen SoundScan, via NARM (National Association of Record Merchandisers). NARM is a non-profit trade association that serves the music content delivery community in a variety of areas including networking, advocacy, information, education and promotion of music.

NARM has a diverse membership. Their core retail membership consists of music wholesalers and retailers, including brick-and-mortar, online and mobile music delivery companies. Furthermore, their membership encompasses distributors, record labels, multimedia suppliers, technology companies, and suppliers of related products and services. Many individual professionals and educators in the music industry are also members of NARM.

NARM's retail members operate thousands of physical, digital and mobile storefronts that account for an estimated 90% of the music sold in the $7 billion dollar per year U.S. music market. Their continued existence is a testament to the fact that the music industry is not only adapting to current changes, but also working actively to advance growth for the industry in the future.

Below is a snapshot list of retail sales in the music industry for the 52-week period December 31, 2007 through December 28, 2008, from data provided by Nielsen SoundScan.

2008 Facts

- Physical music purchases in 2008 reached 1.5 billion units, marking the fourth consecutive year music sales have exceeded 1 billion; 1.4 billion (2007) versus 1.2 billion (2006) versus 1 billion (2005)

- Physical music sales exceeded 65 million units in the final week of 2008, representing the biggest sales week in the history of Nielsen SoundScan. The previous record was Christmas week 2007 with 58.4 million music purchases.

- Overall album sales (including Album and Track Equivalent Album sales) declined 8.5% compared to 2007.

- Total album sales declined 14% compared to 2007.

- Metallica's "Death Magnetic" was the best selling Internet album for the year 2008 with 144,000 downloads sold.

- During 2008, more vinyl albums were purchased (1.88 million) than any other year in the history of Nielsen SoundScan. The previous record was in 2000, with 1.5 million LP album sales.

Note that more than two out of every three vinyl albums were purchased at an independent music store during this year.

Digital Retail Facts

- Digital track sales broke the 1 billion sales mark for the first time with more than 1,070,000,000 digital track sales. The previous record was 844 million digital track purchases during 2007; an increase of 27% over 2007.

☛ Digital album sales reached an all-time high with more than 65 million downloads in 2008; up from 50 million in 2007; an increase of 32% over the previous year.

☛ Note that digital album sales accounted for 15% of total album sales compared to 10% in 2007 and 5.5% in 2006.

☛ In the final reporting week of 2008 the following digital sales records were broken:

☛ Digital track sales surpassed 47.7 million. The previous weekly sales record was 42.9 million, in the week of 12/23 through 12/30 2007. Digital album sales this week broke the two million mark for the first time with sales of 2.4 million sales; breaking the previous record of 1.9 million (12/30/07).

☛ The top 200 digital songs for the week posted an all-time high with 13.6 million sales; breaking the previous record of 11.9 million during the last week of 2007.

☛ The first time that the top-five digital songs (combining all versions of the same song) sold more than 300,000 downloads in a week with Lady Gaga's "Just Dance" selling 419,000. The record for most downloads for a digital song in one week continued to be Flo Rida's "Low" with sales of 467,000 set during the last week of 2007.

☛ 2008 was the first time a digital song broke the 3 million sales mark in a single year. There were two songs that achieved this milestone; Leona Lewis' "Bleeding Love" and Lil Wayne's "Lollipop;" with sales of 3.4 and 3.2 million respectively.

☛ In 2008, there were 19 different digital songs with sales that exceeded 2 million compared to nine in 2007.

☛ 71 Digital songs exceeded the 1 million sales mark for the year, compared to 41 digital songs in 2007, 22 in 2006, and only two digital songs in 2005.

☛ Rihanna was the biggest selling digital artist in 2008 with nearly 10 million track sales compared to Fergie in 2007, who had 7.5 million track sales.

☛ There are more than 450,000 different physical albums that sold at least one copy over the Internet during 2008 compared to 390,000 in 2007.

Bestseller Facts

☛ Lil Wayne's "Tha Carter III" was the biggest selling single album of the year with 2.8 million total sales.

☛ Taylor Swift is the biggest selling solo artist, with sales greater than 4 million units across two releases.

☛ Taylor Swift's "Fearless" and self-titled album finished the year at #3 and #6 respectively with sales of 2.1 and 1.5 million (totalling 4 million). This is the first time in the history of Nielsen SoundScan one artist had two different albums in the Top-10 on the year-end album chart.

☛ AC/DC is the biggest selling group in 2008 with sales of 3.4 million (all physical sales—no digital releases).

COACH'S CORNER: Country is Up—Way Up

As Taylor Swift stands at the top of the list, marking the second time in the last three years that a country artist is the top selling artist for the year. Rascal Flatts was the biggest selling artist in 2006 with 5 million sales. Josh Groban took the honors in 2007 with 4.8 million sales.

Holiday Season Facts (last 6 weeks of year)

☛ Overall album sales during the 2008 holiday season were down 19% as compared to 2007, with sales of just over 80 million.

☛ Album sales during the holiday season accounted for 19% of all album sales for the year.

☛ Digital album sales during the holiday season experienced significant growth over 2007 with an increase of 37% to 9.9 million sales.

Channel Facts

☛ Album sales at non-traditional music outlets (digital, Internet, mail order, venue, non-traditional retailers) hit an all-time high in 2008 with sales breaking the 100 million mark for the first time. Non-traditional is the only strata that experienced album growth over the previous year; with an increase of 15% over 2007. Non-traditional outlets accounted for nearly 25% of all album sales, compared to 18% in 2007, 12% in 2006, 9% in 2005 and 5% in 2004 (4% in 2003). Digital services accounted for 65% of the non-traditional album sales.

☛ The last two weeks of the year produced the two biggest album sales weeks for non-traditional outlets; 3.3 and 3.2 million sales.

☛ The percentage of album sales at mass merchants declined for the second straight year after experiencing year over year growth from 2002–2006. In 2008, 37% of all albums purchased were at a mass-merchant outlet compared to 40% in 2007, 41% in 2006, and 40% in 2005.

☛ Chain music stores accounted for 33% of all album sales in 2008; compared to 36% in 2007; 41% in 2006, 45% in 2005 and 48% in 2004.

☛ Album sales at independent music stores account for 7% of all album sales; up 1 point from a year ago (6% in 2007 and 2006, 7% in 2005 and 9% in 2004).

COACH'S CORNER: Good News, Bad News

Note that independent store sales have had an increase over both 2006 and 2007! Based on these statistics we can see that the retail music industry on the whole is contracting, but there are some encouraging statistics as well. Non-traditional retailer sales were up in 2008 as well as non-traditional retail products, like vinyl.

There are many entities trying to fight the slide of music retail with events like "Record Store Day," which is organized annually by the Coalition of Independent Music Stores (CIMS), Alliance of Independent Music Stores (AIMS), Newbury Comics (27 Stores) and Value Music Concepts (50 Stores). This annual event has created a huge consumer response and broken sales records in independent and small chain stores alike. Many retailers reported sales equal to or greater than the holiday season on this single day. This event has become "Christmas in April" for many of the retailers who are battling the sales decline on the frontlines every day of the year.

Another developing aspect in music retail is the upturn in apparel sales. Music retailers have started to embrace all forms of successful band and artist merchandizing including shirts and sweatshirts, eyewear, footwear, pint glasses, posters, etc.

Digital music has also begun to embrace new technology like "drop cards" (which are like credit cards with a specific link or code that allows you to download digital music) or other digital-based promotions such as "free track giveaways," which require the fan to register their e-mail address for the "free download." These promotional tactics often pay off, as there's a good chance the consumer will revisit their site for future purchases. Furthermore, the digital content provider now has secured another direct contact (your e-mail address) for future marketing and promotions.

As with any industry, the music business is a business first and must remain profitable. If the major labels can't do this, the responsibility will fall to the independent labels. The next decade will see countless changes in how music is sold, and where people buy their music, and if the music business is going to survive and grow, the retail sector in particular must find a way to remain relevant and profitable.

Terrestrial Broadcasting

The roughly 20 years between World War I and World War II were an important time for the music industry. Although there were many advances in radio technology, the development of broadcast advertising didn't take place until the 1930s and 1940s. This development opened the door to composers and musicians who began creating music to underscore the various advertising segments. Over 70 years later, there are still people making a healthy living creating music for advertising. Broadcast advertising helped fuel many new companies and created a whole new set of revenue streams for any band or artist lucky enough to get their music placed in an advertisement.

When radio was first introduced nationally in the 1930s, many people predicted that it would be the end of records and the recording business. Radio was a free medium for anyone to hear music for which they would normally pay. While some of the companies saw radio as a new avenue for promotion, others feared it would cut into profits from record sales and live performances. Many of the major record companies of the era had their major stars sign agreements that they would not appear on radio.

Indeed, the music recording industry saw a severe drop in profits after the introduction of radio. For a while, it appeared as though radio was a legitimate threat to the record industry. Radio ownership grew from two out of five homes in 1931 to four out of five homes in 1938. Meanwhile record sales fell from $75 million in 1929 to $26 million in 1938 (with a low point of $5 million in 1933). It should be noted that the economics of the situation were also greatly affected by the economic turmoil of the Great Depression.

The copyright owners of songs were also concerned they would be adversely affected by the popularity of radio and the "free" music it provided. Fortunately for them, existing copyright law said that the copyright holder for a song had control over all public performances "for profit." The challenge became proving that the radio industry, which was just figuring out for itself how to make money from advertising, was making a profit from the songs.

The test case for the profitability of the radio model was a legal filing brought against Bamberger Department Store in Newark, New Jersey in 1922. Bamberger's was broadcasting music throughout its store on the radio station WOR. No advertisements were heard, except at the beginning of the broadcast when the MC announced "L. Bamberger and Co., One of America's Great Stores, Newark, New Jersey." It was determined through this and previous cases (such as a major lawsuit against Shanley's Restaurant) that Bamberger was using the songs for commercial gain, thus making it a public performance for profit, which meant the copyright owners were due payment for the broadcast of the works.

With this court ruling, The American Society of Composers, Authors and Publishers (ASCAP) began collecting licensing fees from radio stations in 1923. The initial sum was $230 for all music protected under ASCAP, but for larger stations the price soon ballooned up to $5,000. Edward Samuel's reports in his book *The Illustrated Story of Copyright* that "radio and TV licensing represents the single greatest source of revenue for ASCAP and its composers." The average member of ASCAP received about $150-$200 per work per year, or about $5,000–$6,000 for all of a member's compositions. Not long after the Bamberger ruling, ASCAP had to once again defend their right to charge fees in 1924.

With this milestone case, it became obvious that the music industry was a means for many people to prosper. Radio in particular was the sole source for the average American family's news, entertainment, and sports from its inception in the early part of the 20th century until it was replaced by television in the 1950s. With this direct conduit into American homes, music became big business for the few major companies who controlled content delivery at that time. This meant that the record company who had recorded an artist could now control the radio performances and thereby could literally "break" new music.

This allowed companies who had the big artists of the day to not only dominate the airwaves, but also send consumers scurrying to the nearest place to buy music. With the advent of the home turntable, the major companies could now break a single on radio, and then reap the profits from the artist's fans rushing out to buy the album (first in the form of 78s and later LPs and singles).

This upturn gained speed after World War II, when people returning home from the war wanted new entertainment. The bands and artists of this time enjoyed some of the largest financial successes in the history of the music business. Artists like Frank Sinatra and Bing Crosby, two notable examples of "artists turned icon," as radio carried their music across the country, and later all over the world.

Another pivotal shift in the music industry was the slow transition from a totally "aural" medium to an aural *and* visual medium. This shift was a result of the widespread acceptance of the television in American homes. Looks became incredibly important, and the emergence of "heart-throbs" like Elvis Presley came to dominate the industry, and continue to do so to this day. This meant that if someone wanted to be successful in the music industry, they would have to be attractive (or at least interesting looking) to achieve mainstream success.

This time was also incredibly important as it saw the emergence of the radio host or MC. These MCs became incredibly important to the major music companies as they could inspire listeners to do almost anything. Their goal was simple: Get people to buy records, attend shows, and support their artists and bands. These hosts were most powerful from the 1950s through the 1990s. Radio spots was owned by the highest bidder and advertising dollars controlled the commercials, but it was the MC and/or program director who controlled the content the listening audience would hear. This birthed a very dangerous, but all too familiar condition referred to as "payola", or, paying to have your music played on the radio.

COACH'S CORNER: Payola

From the mid-1950s until the late-1980s, radio stations were paid—often by bribes or gifts from major labels, which could be as large as cars or other valuables—to play certain music. This marks a time during which music industry gained a bad reputation and lost the trust of the American people. The industry's most profitable years were still to come, but there was now a question in every listeners mind, "Is this music good, or did someone pay for me to hear it?" This question marked a line between commercial music stations (who sold advertising as its only real revenue stream) and college and community radio that was generally listener sponsored. As a result, many people flocked to the college and community radio stations simply because they felt that they could trust programming. Although commercial stations had a much wider listening audience, the smaller stations were able to develop a die-hard core listenership who valued the fact that their station's new music was played based on merit and musical content rather than advertising dollars. This also meant that independent stations were able to embrace a much wider spectrum of styles than commercial stations.

The late 1990s gave birth to a new technology, which used cable rather than radio waves to deliver music to its audience. DMX and XM radio were born as "cable-only" radio that allowed the listeners to view music genres and listen to music without commercial interruption. Because these services were based on a subscription model, there was no need for traditional advertising revenue. These services grew in 2000 and expanded their subscription model to provide wireless access to these broadcasts in cars and on mobile devices.

The 21st century saw the emergence of podcasting and the iPod as well as an entirely new group of players in radio. Digital music and streaming digital radio have replaced terrestrial radio for many audiences all over the world. Further diluting the content delivery pool are new Websites like Last FM, Pandora, and Slacker Radio that function as radio stations for millions of listeners. The future is uncertain for traditional radio stations, but many are making the change from broadcasting over traditional radio waves to fiber-optic Internet cables. Programming which was until very recently only available to local listeners is now available worldwide.

15

The Business Plan Primer

The business plan is one of the most important documents a business owner or potential business owner will ever write. It details the specifics of the management, marketing, operations, and finances of a new venture and allows for the owner to plan for and manage the possible objectives and outcomes related to opening any business. This document allows for an owner to understand and clearly present how the business will operate, including financial projections of potential profits, start-up costs, and possible contingency plans and risk assessment.

COACH'S CORNER: You are the Business

One of the biggest mistakes a band, artist, or producer makes is missing the fact that you are your business. You are what is being hired for the gig—whether it's a j-o-b or not. You are in the business of selling you—your talents, your time, your ideas—all of it. Having a business plan for yourself is tremendously important. Not everyone is an entrepreneur (some of us just want a j-o-b), but if you plan to be the for-hire gun, you're an entrepreneur!

Building Your Blueprint For Success

The business plan provides a blueprint for how the business will achieve profitability. This is particularly important to potential investors who will want to know how and when they will see their Return On Investment (ROI). A good business plan also allows for an owner to set various long and short-term goals that will

DVD-ROM Supporting Documentation
Indie Artist Timeline and Worksheet for New Releases.xls

become benchmarks for the growth of the business, which are key point to an investor knowing whether or not the plan is working.

The first phase of writing a business plan is a "feasibility study." This allows you to better understand the potential of your proposed venture. This entails considering the specific market for the type of business you propose, and the general market conditions surrounding your venture. This study could include focus groups and surveys of everyday people who might use your product or service. It could also include a review of the competition and a simple study of risks related to the business. Once this study is complete, and you are ready to move forward, the next step is to create a schedule or timeline for your plan.

A tool that many strategic planners use is called a SWOT (Strengths, Weakness, Opportunities, and Threats) analysis. This breakdown creates an introductory overview that gives you a preliminary understanding of your business and the environment in which it operates.

Figure 15: *An example of a typical SWOT analysis.*

Strengths

① Unique Product – little competition for similar products.

② Limited Cost of Goods – translates to high profit margins.

③ Diverse Staff – flexibility if a unique job or opportunity presents.

④ Manageable Overhead – little change in fixed costs makes profit predictions consistent.

⑤ Location – Lots of visibility creates affordable marketing.

Weaknesses

① Poor Cash flow – Little predictability of cash flow threatens payroll and Accounts Payable.

② Growth before Profitability – need to grow into new business siphons cash away from expenses and payroll.

③ Unfocused Business Development – Chasing many opportunities at once with a small staff makes for poor customer contact and service.

④ Unrealistic Goals – In growth industries, dreaming is easy. Little cash flow and poor focus yields unfocused results that don't match the goals.

Opportunities

① Overall Industry Growth – growing industry means growing customer base (B2C and B2B).

② Developing New Technologies – High tech creates affordable products and increased efficiencies.

③ Consumer Confidence – repeat business!

④ Industry Relationships – Depth of network creates new and hidden opportunities.

Threats

① Overall Industry Downturn – is this growth sustainable? Spending into a growth of the company might over grow expenses with a sudden shift against revenue.

② Increased Cost Of Goods – Current low COGS might change with increased technology. New tech creates poor competition and increases expenses.

③ Damaged Reputation – Poor focus on goals and customer service yields damaged reputation which slows growth and repeat business.

By filling out this basic study, a business owner should be able to clearly define the important aspects that will be detailed in the full business plan. By using this simple chart, the owner hopes to identify (and hopefully eliminate) threats and weaknesses while capitalizing on strengths and opportunities. Once the feasibility study and a SWOT analysis have been completed, you are ready to begin drafting your business plan.

How Long Will Writing the Business Plan Take?

Writing the first sections of a business plan could take anywhere from a few days to a few weeks. Some people take months just to spell out the mission statement and the executive summary. It might take five months to write a good business plan, and if successful, it should keep someone interested for five minutes. It's a good idea to write what comes most easily to you first. Work on the harder parts once you have a few pages under your belt. Most small business owners can write their mission statement in a matter of days, while it might take a few months to really develop the operations or marketing sections.

When you have completed every section, go back and carefully edit the document into a presentable package. The average plan should be between 20 and 40 single-spaced pages. It may also include various spreadsheets that detail timelines and financials, as well as basic images, logos and appendices.

What's most important here are two things—being right and being first. The plan has to work, first and foremost. If the plan stinks, who in their right mind would fund it? Who would support it? Having well-researched and supported information is HUGE. To this end, I suggest you take your time and get it right—the first time. Nothing is worse than presenting a great plan to a great partner/investor only to find out that your "great plan" ain't so great. Not only did you lose their interest, you now realize that you have more work to do.

The second issue, being first, has more to do with what we call "speed to market." The general rule is, "first to market wins." You and a competitor might both see an opportunity at the same time. You both develop business plans and you both seek investors. However, your competition beat you to the punch and is already up and running. Now, when you go to seek investors, you're likely to be presented with the question—"Business X already does this—why is your idea better?"

This is a valid question but one you might not be able to answer—Business X didn't exist when you studied the competition and how you plan to deal with them isn't in the plan. Now, you'll have to go back and re-study them and decide if you do have a niche that they don't offer. AKA, you've got to go back to the drawing board.

COACH'S CORNER: Being First Isn't Everything

Speed to market is a big issue but not the only issue. Take for example the study of VHS versus Beta in the '70s and '80s. Beta is a much higher quality video format than VHS was but VHS hit the market first. It was also easier to use and much cheaper and as such, took the public market away from Beta, relegating Beta to professional use. This should sound a lot like the debate between CDs and MP3s—first to market is important, but convenience in this case is the winner. You should think about how your business will be received by the marketplace—even though you're first, are you the best? It could be that you've left a BIG hole in your plan and the next guy along sees that. You'll be first, but they'll be best. In this case, you can watch your early victory disappear all too quickly.

To this end, there are two general rules that can be borrowed from the military:

The "6 Ps: Prior Planning Prevents Piss-Poor Performance" and "a good plan today is better than a great plan tomorrow."

Who Is the Target of this Document?

How in-depth your plan should be is largely dependent on the reader of the document. If you are constructing the document strictly for yourself, you should be somewhat in-depth but do not have to go to the level of detail you would if the reader is a potential investor. Again, it needs to be good today, not great tomorrow. If your end user is a bank or other funding source, then be prepared to create a long and complex document—they'll need to see great. Good might not be good enough.

If the target audience is a venture capital firm, understand that they receive hundreds of business plans a month and if it is not presented in a complete and succinct manor, it will never get past the first consideration. Again, it should be great. If your target is an "angel" investor such as a family member or colleague (they look like an angel with the money they bring in—insert choir sound here . . .), it may be beneficial for you to include images or sketches to keep them interested. There are many companies who do both a written plan and a visual presentation to complement the written version.

Be it a visual or a strong oral presentation, many a deal has been made because a presenter's personality or charisma sold the idea. Nothing is worse than working for months on a great business plan, but failing to connect with the potential investor due to bad presentation. A successful presentation takes rehearsal. Don't try to present an idea, no matter how close it is to your heart, without preparing in advance for the actual presentation.

When the time comes to formally present your business plan, arrive at the meeting dressed accordingly and well rehearsed. Bring copies of the business plan for everyone attending the meeting. If you are doing an audio/visual presentation, think through any possible technical problems that could occur. Make sure that they can connect your laptop, or have the correct program to open your file. Technical glitches can undermine an otherwise great presentation.

If the presentation takes place outside of a traditional office environment, keep the presentation simple. Allow the details to reach the audience with the written document, while using the A/V presentation to convey broad concepts and images that will impress or "wow" the viewers. If you do your job, the attendees should be anxious to dive into your plan. If you lose them in the presentation, the intricacies of your plan will likely never be read. People tend to invest in people.

Since you're the one they're investing in, be sure to look the part. That means your plan can't have any silliness. Please—no spelling errors, grammatical errors or just plain misuse of the language. Involving others in the editing process is often hugely beneficial. Once you've proofread your own document thoroughly, pass it to someone in your inner circle for further editing. Before doing so, you should require that they sign a *Non-Disclosure Agreement* (NDA) to protect any sensitive information therein. An example of a NDA is seen in **Figure 16**.

The NDA is a one-page document that spells out that you (the discloser) are disclosing sensitive, confidential facts to the reader. The reader must sign the statement stating that they will not communicate the information they are reading to anyone who has not signed the same agreement, and will under no circumstance try to engage in, or open a similar business without being subject to legal action.

By defining these terms upfront, there is no way for someone to legally read your business plan and subsequently use the information to start another company in your line of business. This document is typically delivered as a separate document to be signed and held by both parties. Deliver this agreement to anyone who might view your document and keep signed non-disclosure agreements in a safe and secure location.

GENERAL NONDISCLOSURE AGREEMENT

This is an agreement, effective _____, between [NAME OF DISCLOSER] (the "Discloser") and [NAME OF RECIPIENT] (the "Recipient"), in which Discloser agrees to disclose, and Recipient agrees to receive, certain trade secrets of Discloser on the following terms and conditions:

1. Trade Secrets: Recipient understands and acknowledges that Discloser's trade secrets consist of information and materials that are valuable and not generally known by Discloser's competitors or other third parties. Discloser's trade secrets include:

(a) Any and all information concerning Discloser's current, future or proposed business model, operations or plans.

(b) Information and materials relating to Discloser's accounting, financial condition, projections, budget and marketing, including, but not limited to, financial statements and projections, budget projections, marketing plans, sales data, cost and pricing information, customer lists and proposed partners and customers.

(c) Information of the type described above which Discloser obtained from another party and which Discloser treats as confidential, whether or not owned or developed by Discloser.

(d) Information of the type described above relating to any affiliate company or business of Discloser (including all owners, executives, employees, clients, customers, business partners and agents thereof).

2. Purpose of Disclosure: Recipient shall make use of Discloser's trade secrets only for the purpose of evaluating a potential business relationship with Disclosure.

3. Nondisclosure: In consideration of Discloser's disclosure of its trade secrets to Recipient, Recipient agrees that it will treat Discloser's trade secrets with the same degree of care and safeguards that it takes with its own trade secrets, but in no event less than a reasonable degree of care. Recipient agrees that, without Discloser's prior written consent, Recipient will not:

(a) disclose Discloser's trade secrets to any third party;

(b) make or permit to be made copies or other reproductions of Discloser's trade secrets; or

(c) make any commercial use of the trade secrets.

Recipient will not disclose Discloser's trade secrets to Recipient's employees, agents and consultants unless: (1) they have a need to know the information in connection with their employment or consultant duties; and (2) they personally agree in writing to be bound by the terms of this Agreement.

4. Return of Materials: Upon Discloser's request, Recipient shall promptly (within 5 days) return all original materials provided by Discloser and any copies, notes or other documents in Recipient's possession pertaining to Discloser's trade secrets.

5. Term: This Agreement and Recipient's duty to hold Discloser's trade secrets in confidence shall remain in effect until the above-described trade secrets are no longer trade secrets or until Discloser sends Recipient written notice releasing Recipient from this Agreement, whichever occurs first.

6. No Rights Granted: Recipient understands and agrees that this Agreement does not constitute a grant or an intention or commitment to grant any right, title or interest in Discloser's trade secrets to Recipient.

7. Warranty: Discloser warrants that it has the right to make the disclosures under this Agreement. NO OTHER WARRANTIES ARE MADE BY DISCLOSER UNDER THIS AGREEMENT. ANY INFORMATION DISCLOSED UNDER THIS AGREEMENT IS PROVIDED "AS IS."

8. Injunctive Relief: Recipient recognizes and acknowledges that any breach or threatened breach of this Agreement by Recipient may cause Discloser irreparable harm for which monetary damages may be inadequate. Recipient agrees, therefore, that Discloser shall be entitled to an injunction to restrain Recipient from such breach or threatened breach. Nothing in this Agreement shall be construed as preventing Discloser from pursuing any remedy at law or in equity for any breach or threatened breach of this Agreement.

9. Attorney Fees: If any legal action arises relating to this Agreement, the prevailing party shall be entitled to recover all court costs, expenses and reasonable attorney fees.

10. Modifications: All additions or modifications to this Agreement must be made in writing and must be signed by both parties to be effective.

11. No Agency: This Agreement does not create any agency or partnership relationship between the parties.

12. Applicable Law: This Agreement is made under, and shall be construed according to, the laws of the State of California.

[Signature Page to Follow]

Discloser: [NAME OF DISCLOSER]

By: _____
    (signature)

_____
(typed or printed name)

Title: _____

Date: _____

Recipient: [NAME OF RECIPIENT]

By: _____
    (signature)

_____
(typed or printed name)

Title: _____

Date: _____

Figure 16: *A generic NDA, which should be signed by anyone with whom you discuss your business ideas or plans.*

Once you have two or three "red-lined" versions of the final plan, compare the documents and evaluate whose changes are better. When you have a finished text, start creating a multimedia presentation that incorporates the text and images that make up the business plan. Do not share this presentation with any potential investors or partners until is absolutely complete (AND the NDA is signed!). It's often a good idea to invite a few people you trust to watch the presentation and give you honest feedback before presenting to a potential partner/investor.

No matter where you are in the lifespan of your business, if you've formed your business using a business plan, you will have to spend time revisiting the document and presentation. This is why the business plan is often referred to as a "living document." Circumstances, market conditions, and the world around you will always change. In order to adapt, you must revisit and update the content at least once a year. Eventually you might develop sub-business plans that target new aspects of business development relevant to the future of your company.

"Do's and Don'ts" Of Composing and Presenting Your Plan

☞   Be honest. If you lie on your résumé and someone discovers it, you will lose every shred of credibility you ever had.

☞   Where possible, write in the third person. Do not use "I" or "we." This will help you to focus on what you are saying from an outside perspective.

☞   Use active and dynamic verbs to lead the reader from one concept to another. Make them feel like they are on the "rollercoaster" with you.

☞   Use language appropriate for your audience. If you get lost in details or use too much slang or jargon, you might lose the reader's attention.

☞   Use tables and charts to define how your profit and expenses might develop. Use visuals wherever possible to paint a picture of what aspects you think will excite reader/viewers.

☛ Avoid using redundant language or statements that will make the reader think you are "fluffing" up the information you are presenting.

How to Begin

Having a great idea (at least—*you* think so . . .) and having it work are NOT the same thing. Running a business is a LOT of work—having a great idea is not. Be sure that you're up for the task of writing the plan and doing the work. Weak or lazy business plans indicate to someone that you are weak and lazy yourself. I'm guessing this isn't the impression you want to make.

Keep in mind that this book is the *beginning* of writing business plans. This is a monumental task for even the simplest business and will likely be the most important document of your career. We're going to go through the high-level stuff, with some attention paid to analyzing the market to see if your great idea even fits. The details of a business plan are described later in the section "Writing a Business Plan" by Paul Terry. Feel free to skip ahead to that section then come back here to begin to apply it to our industry.

When first approaching your business plan, write what you feel is the easy stuff first. The summary statement and mission statement should come easily if you write with the passion you have for your idea. Both of these sections should be written from your heart, without focusing on the "day-to-day" details. Once you've completed your summary and mission statements, you'll need to approach the plan from a more technical perspective, focusing on topics like operations and marketing. As these sections start coming together, you can then begin work on the more "heady" sections.

COACH'S CORNER: A Simple Test

If you lack the focus and discipline to write a business plan, you lack the focus and discipline to launch and run a successful business. You know it, I know it and worse, the investor knows it. Most investors invest in the people first and the plan second. The plan can change—the people can't (at least, not easily).

If you are a "talker" (the person who got all those people to come out to your gigs), you might want to tackle the marketing plan first. To do so, you need to first define the scope of the business and how it will actually run. Once this has been established, you can then focus on marketing. If you are an introverted person, you may want to consult a professional for help on the marketing aspect of the plan.

Before writing your business plan, you must define the audience for the plan. Is it a bank, an angel investor or a venture capital firm? Is it someone in your family? Is it you? Your business plan should be as in-depth and detailed as it can possibly be, making sure to get every point addressed. This includes financial projections and start-up costs, as well as a timeline for growth and expansion. If the main goal is to raise money, your plan should account for exactly how and when you intend to pay back the loan.

If your end user is you, and you're writing the business plan to create a "game-plan" for your company's growth, take your time and cover as much as you can. Write as much as possible now and edit it later. This plan will ultimately be your roadmap to success, so the more time and effort you put into your plan, the better.

Writing a business plan is a long process. It could take anywhere from a week to several years to have a final, implementable plan that will take you from an idea to "Doors Open." Once you have opened your business, you must treat your business plan as a living document that needs to be nurtured and tweaked with the times. Be sure to revisit your business plan often, first to see how well you are executing your plans, and secondly, to assess the industry around you and make changes to your scope and core as needed.

Most business plans have six sections that describe the business with as much detail as possible. They are:

☛ Executive Summary (with mission statement)

☛ The Business Overview

☛ Marketing Plan

☛ The Management Team

☛ Financial Plan

☛ Analysis and Business Development (the Future)

Again, this will be covered in more detail in Paul Terry's text but I'll give you an overview of the "big picture sections"—the Summary, the Overview and the Analysis sections.

Executive Summary

Every business plan should start with a page or two that outlines the most fundamental details such as company name, address, contact numbers, e-mail address, Website, and the name and title of any principals of the company or corporation. After this, launch directly to the executive summary.

The executive summary and the included mission statement are the nuts and bolts of any good business plan. These sections of your plan can be defined as the "head" and "heart" of the business plan. The heart is the mission statement, which in a few sentences defines the objective of the business. You need to take care in writing this section, as it will define your business for years to come. It is the mission statement that wows people and draws them in based on the company's overall value proposition. Simple is better, in many cases the most effective mission statements are those that really strike a personal chord with the reader.

COACH'S CORNER: The Value of a Few Words

You should strive to inspire people with this section right out of the gate. Although many serious investors will start by reading the executive summary to get a picture of the business, plenty of venture capital and "angel" investors will first want to understand the heart of the business before diving into the nuts and bolts of how the business will operate. The executive summary may be the most important few sentences you write about the business, so take your time and make it great!

The executive summary is the "head" of the business plan. This section is a snapshot of the entire business, including financials, marketing, operations, and a history of the main partners. This is the core of your business plan. The executive statement should take the longest to complete. As opposed to the mission statement (which should generally be between two and five paragraphs), the executive summary must be a fairly lengthy section. The executive summary could be considered a "mini" business plan in its own right. You will need to have almost all your research completed before you start to flesh out this section, so it will likely be the *last* section you write.

The goal of a well-prepared executive summary should be to draw the investor into the business proposal. The mission statement should do the same thing, but a serious investor will read the executive summary about your operations and your business structure to understand how much investment is needed. If they are interested, they should finish it feeling like they want more. These sections should engage the reader and keep them reading into the body of the plan. Many people to whom you present your plan may never read beyond those two sections, so they must be engrossing and dynamic. By creating a proper mission statement and executive summary, you are giving your business a chance to get funded.

The Business Overview

The description of business section should be as simple and straightforward as possible. Describe your proposed business and how it will operate. You do not need to go into great detail about actual operations, as you will cover that subject in-depth in the operations section of the plan. The description of business section of the plan should be a basic overview of what the business does on a day-to-day basis.

You may also use this section to define how your business is different from others. Be prepared to write about things like the business structure itself—a corporation, a partnership, a sole-proprietorship, etc. Who will be the manager or managing partners and who will you employee initially? This section may also provide the reader with background information about the specific business in which your company is looking to be engaged.

Market Analysis

Knowing the Market for Your Business

Before starting a business, it is only logical to learn from those who are currently operating a business like the one you envision. If there's no one out there doing what you want to do, maybe there's a reason—perhaps your idea has been tried and doesn't work.

Visionary entrepreneurs look to create opportunities where none exist. This recipe has potential for huge success as well as huge failure. Before creating something from nothing, one must get a sense of the landscape. Are there large costs in developing this business? Is there a customer base for this business? Will the revenue repay the start-up costs in a timely fashion while also paying employees' salaries and monthly overhead?

Truth be told, it is much harder to open a business that has no real competition because there is no prior model from which to learn. The key to understanding your first entrepreneurial endeavor relates directly to knowing and understanding the market for your business, if there is one.

Market research information has traditionally been expensive and difficult to obtain. Thus, many startup companies simply cannot afford to hire others to determine the validity of their business idea in the market prior to opening shop. Large companies pay big bucks to understand their customers' needs and wants, but small companies have to rely on other methods. Customer satisfaction surveys can be tedious, but also provide good benchmarks of the marketplace. Polling the man-on-the-street is another. Today, joining online groups and forums and reading between the lines of others' conversations is a great (and free!) way to start to determine if your idea has a market.

The Internet has been hugely influential in leveling the playing field—it makes research much easier by watching other like-minded businesses. It has also helped people run their businesses while living or working in remote locations. Once you know who else is out there (no matter where they are if they're an online business), you can determine where you fit into the business marketplace. This first step (which will be explained more later) is called your *value proposition*—what is the value of your proposition to the market. Once you have your value proposition, it should be fairly easy to understand the other side of the market—your *competition profile.*

By researching those businesses that have come before you, you can learn from the mistakes of the competition. In doing so, you can define and develop a basic set of guidelines, focusing your energy on techniques that were successful for other people. You can also see which ideas may have gone unrealized, or were under-appreciated when someone else tried to get them off the ground. Using this knowledge, you can create a plan to grow your idea and let it take shape, without replicating the failures that held others back.

Who's Your Customer? B2B or B2C?

Knowing the market for your business stems from the need to know your end user. Identifying your target client or customer is an important factor that helps determine how many (and what kind of) people your product or service will reach. Your end users will be grouped by various traits or demographics, called *verticals (or vertical markets)*, and by knowing which verticals appeal to, you will be able to better understand how your business works.

Large corporations hire teams of people to perform market research on how people act and why they buy what they buy. They create reports to help the sales teams understand their target audience and end user. This information may also help the company understand how much a prospective client or customer would pay for their products or services. Still other companies hire outside consultants to determine how to advertise to perspective customers, or to establish which products or services are most marketable before spending money in development.

For independent businesspersons looking to better understand their market or potential customer base, it has never been as easy to find this information as it is today, using the Internet and/or by creating small, personalized focus groups, like social network groups. Finding a few people you trust to represent the core audience or target market for your service or product can help you to better understand the broader demographic without the expense of hiring a market research team to analyze the industry.

Each member of the focus group is going to have different opinions. Your ability to poll each one, in front of others or in secret, will give you very valuable and insightful information, which will become the foundation of the marketing section of your business plan. You might find that many of the individuals that you thought would be customers are not interested in your idea. However, many of these same individuals work for companies that would be interested.

For example, your business may be a company that sells to other businesses (B-to-B, often shortened as "B2B") as opposed to selling directly to consumers (B-to-C or "B2C"). This determination is important to know because the tactics used by a business that is selling B2C will often be different than the strategies you would use to sell your product or service B2B.

If your business is B2B, you can focus your advertising on specialized publications and Websites that target your potential business customers. This is a much smaller focus than a B2C business, which could save in marketing costs. B2C businesses need a much larger marketing budget than B2B businesses that only place a few ads in trade magazines or on specific Websites that cater directly to their type of business.

A B2B will spend time and money attending industry events and joining groups and organizations that support and affect their type of business. This means if you are a music producer who wants to create music for films, joining various groups or societies who work with film composers would be more effective than putting an ad in your local free paper that says "I will score your film! Cheap!" (which may actually hurt your chances of success—who wants cheap music?).

If you are a B2C business, there are myriad ways you can reach potential customers that didn't exist even a few years ago. In addition to the usual traditional media like television, newspapers, magazines, and billboards, there are now thousands of outlets for promotions available across the Internet. There is an ever growing, constantly changing parade of social and music networking platforms and Websites that allow businesses of any size to drive sales by advertising to a very targeted or wide demographic, for much less money than traditional advertising campaigns might cost.

Of course, there are still tried and tested methods like posters and flyers, which are inexpensive and easy to manufacture and distribute. These raise an awareness of your products and services, and can grow your business without the high price of a television ad campaign. There are plenty of businesses that create cool, low budget informational videos that get thousands of people's attention with a 5-minute clip on YouTube.

It is possible that once you have established your business, you may change the focus or the core of your business to engage a different sector of the customer base. For example, if after two years of building a record label, you've been successful in marketing your products to fans and through your own Website, but now you want to get your physical product into stores nationally. This has changed your business from a B2C to both a B2C and a B2B business. Now, not only are you marketing your product to your fans, but also to a distributor (a business) who needs to market your products to stores (other businesses).

This same type of business transition could occur for someone who starts a company to make music for films. After some success placing their music in a few TV spots and motion pictures, they realize that there is a consumer-level demand for their music. The composer then presses 1,000 CDs and sells them through their Website, other online retailers like iTunes etc. Eventually there is enough demand to get those CDs into local stores. Now this business has turned its core focus from a B2B to more of a B2C business. Many times businesses will settle and grow as both a B2B and B2C business, depending on where they find demand for their goods or services.

Marketing today is different than ever before. Today's technology provides nearly endless possibilities if you understand your business and your end user. With this technology, you can put together an affordable, effective marketing campaign right from your computer. This may include:

☛ Digital Public Relations (PR)

☛ Social Networking

☛ Banner Ads

☛ Search Engine Optimization (SEO)

☛ E-Newsletter

☛ Ad Word Campaigns.

Finally, once you have identified your end users and pitched them your product or service, you can then ask for feedback about their experience. Is your product or service a good value to them? Was it received in a timely manner? Would they recommend your company to a friend? These questions play a part not only in reaching potential customers initially, but also in retaining them as long-term clients.

What's Missing From The Market?

People often discover ways to grow their business by looking at the market and identifying what is missing. For each small offshoot of a standard business model, there are countless people saying "That product would be so cool if . . ." or "I really wish someone would make this . . ." There are many reasons for a successful or failed business, but to be profitable with your own model, you have to explore the market as a consumer of your type of product or service.

Identifying any missing components of *your* business will not only make your business better, but will also force you to examine the business climate for your company.

Once your initial research phase has been completed, you can then move onto the next round of exploration—focus groups. Listening to your focus groups' responses to your newfound information and learning what they think might be missing from your particular business or industry will give you a better understanding of the business climate that you seek to enter. From this perspective you will gain a much more accurate idea of how your business might prosper if you include some missing elements that your competition doesn't offer.

COACH'S CORNER: Lesson From a Pieman

A simple analogy is a small town baker who makes and sells pies. He has no employees and very low overhead. Down the street, a large supermarket opens and they have a huge bakery section that offers dozens of types of pies, cakes and breads. The baker sees this selection, and without any thought expands his offerings and begins to make cakes and breads to compete. His pies suffer, and because he had always been known for the quality of his pies, his overall business suffers. Eventually, the people who came for the pies find that the supermarket's pies are now better and cheaper. If the baker had continued with his core business (pies) and not followed his competition (cakes and breads), he could have broadened his appeal by creating new pie flavors, and his business could have potentially prospered rather than failed. So the moral of this story is: Do what you're best at and don't abandon your business model because of the fear of competition.

Research should always play a definitive role in making decisions about your business. Without proper research you cannot make informed judgments about the direction of your company. This holds true throughout the many stages of businesses growth, but foremost in the planning stage. By understanding who else is out there doing what you plan to do (or by discovering through research that your proposed model does not yet exist), you will have better prepared yourself for success.

Who *Is* Your Competition?

Anyone who tells you they don't have any competition just hasn't looked around enough. Every business has some level of competition or shared customer base. It may be that you share the same core business model or audience, or perhaps someone actually makes the same product as you do. One of the first steps in bringing an idea to market is to analyze the competition to see if there's even room for you in the market.

The first step in assessing your competition is to make a list of five or six different companies who are in the same field or industry as your proposed business. Sort them into a few basic categories like "Bigger Than Me," "Smaller Than Me," "Local," or "National." Some of this data is available for purchase through a service such as Dunn and Bradstreet (www.dnb.com/us). Next, analyze the competition and examine their vendors. This will help you understand how much it costs them to operate their business. Can you find others to do it better? Cheaper? Both?

For example, consider a record label. Who are their artists or bands? What studios do they use? How much marketing and promotion do they do? What are their distribution channels? Is the product available physically and digitally? Do they have good press? How much is their retail sale price? Many of these questions can be answered by simply going online and checking out a few links. These answers should be collected into a spreadsheet that will foster the analysis of multiple competitors simultaneously.

Let's look at an example.

Your dream is to open a recording studio in a big city where there are 20 other full service studios in a 10-mile radius. To be successful, you will have to stand out, but many of these other studios have great reputations and a long history. How do they run their business? What are their facilities like and what they offer to their clients? What kind of gear do they have? Who is running the board at the sessions? Can you get an industry standard product from these studios? What are their rates?

The research will make it clear who is succeeding and who is not and with just a few hours of research (and no out-of-pocket costs), you can paint a picture of your direct competition.

In this process, if you confine your research to Internet searches and anonymous phone inquiries, your competitors won't even know you're starting a competing business. They will often provide you with many of the details you need to create a competition profile for your business plan. By defining and understanding the competition prior to starting your business, you will maximize your chances at success.

Competition will change as your business grows. A small local business can grow into a large regional business, and eventually could become a national company. For the purposes of a business plan, do not put yourself in a field of competitors you cannot compete with. If you are starting a record label do not list one of your competitors as Sony or MCA, but rather pick some smaller independents that are similar to you in size and genre. If you are an entry-level producer, do not list your competition as Dr. Dre and Kanye West, but as some lower-level producers who are still making a living from production.

COACH'S CORNER: Keeping it in Perspective

It is important to maintain perspective throughout this process. One day you may be bigger than Kanye or Dre, but no matter how successful you become, humility, perspective and business savvy will always be fundamental to your continued success. Look at other businesses as fellow players who you should respect and learn from. This does not mean lay down for them, but rather that you should recognize that they are established companies with a track record of success and profits to back it up.

Just as important as identifying your end user or who your competition might be is defining your niche within the industry. A niche can be defined as a place, employment, status, or activity for which a person or thing is best suited. In practical terms, it is often a specific market within the scope of a much broader industry. A good example of a niche within the music business is a record label or recording studio. The music business is an enormous industry (actually part of the bigger entertainment industry), with tens of thousands of different types of businesses that make up the whole business of music.

Simply put: What is your place in the bigger industry? A niche market is defined as a subset of the market in which a specific product is focused. The market niche dictates the specific product features aimed at satisfying specific market needs. The better you understand where your business fits in the market, the better you'll be able to cater specifically to your potential clients or customers.

What's Your Value Proposition?

Simply stated, a value proposition is what you or your company provides a customer over the competition—what is the value of doing business with you? The more specific your value proposition is the better. The information presented by businesses in advertisements is a direct reflection of their value proposition.

Here are a few examples of weak value propositions—(and what they *really* mean to a customer):

☛ It's the most technologically advanced and robust system on the market! (This can be interpreted as difficult to use and support)

☛ We improve communication and morale! (How can you prove this?)

☛ My product was rated the best-in-class by leading authorities! (That's great, but how does this help me?)

These value propositions are weak because they're too general and do not convey any detailed information. Just like résumé writing, action verbs and results are what really sink into a customer's mind when choosing a business—or an employee, for that matter! If one is going to create an advertising campaign or even put their value proposition on a Website, it is in that company's best interest to present a concise statement that can be easily understood by the end-user. Making false claims in your value proposition will ultimately backfire when your customer base becomes dissatisfied, as your product did not live up to their expectations.

Strong value propositions deliver tangible results. And are interpreted by customers as:

☛ Increased revenues (increased profit)

☛ Faster time to market (beat the competition)

☛ Improved operational efficiency (decreased costs and increased profit)

☛ Increased market share (more customers)

☛ Higher quality product/experience (higher sales price and increased revenue)

A good value proposition does not focus solely on the product's features, functions, performance, or pricing. Basing your company's value proposition solely on product attributes lacks the development of a personal relationship with the end-user. Many experts agree that this relationship is the greatest value you can offer to a customer. Highlighting your company's stellar reputation, outstanding customer service, integrity and trustworthiness will go a long way in making a lasting impression on the consumer.

If you can clearly answer the following questions in a way that is meaningful to your customer, you will have gone a long way in developing a strong value proposition.

☛ Do you help your customers increase their revenue?

☛ Do you help your customers decrease their costs?

☛ Do you help your customer increase their profitability?

☛ Do you help your customer better respond to the needs of their customers, and to new opportunities that might be presented by their customers?

☛ Do you help your customers improve their productivity?

☛ Do you help your customers improve their business cycle time/speed?

☛ Do you help your customers improve the satisfaction, retention, and growth of their customers?

☛ Do you help your customers improve their quality?

☛ Do you help your customers improve the satisfaction of their employees?

16

Finding Opportunities in Tough Times

This a tough time for the traditional music industry, yet there are a numerous positive indicators that herald a growth in independent music as a result of the proliferation of digital distribution means. Artists and producers can enjoy low-cost entry to the marketplace through affordable production tools and affordable marketing/sales channels.

There is still, however, the need for these artists and producers to recognize that the artistry that they promote is still them. As such, these artists are in the business of being themselves and, like any good business, a plan should be created to seek out customers. The business plan, while potentially boring, is a key ingredient to one's success in the digital music business. Additionally, understanding where you sit in the market overall will give you a much better understanding of who your customers are and how to get them to buy your product or service.

To get much deeper on business plans, read on to Paul Terry's section. He'll cover all the details of a business plan. Keep in mind that having the focus and discipline to write a plan shows that you have the focus and discipline to run that business. Since that business will likely be you, it is extremely important that you buckle down and ask (and answer) the hard questions before you spend your money and time fighting an unwinnable battle.

Section 4

Creating the Business Plan

by Paul Terry

Introduction

One of the key themes of this book is recognizing the vast opportunities that exist within today's changing music and audio production industry. The idea is to search within that change for the opportunity—the "hidden potential" described in Gregory J. Gordon's writing earlier. In times where the market changes, individuals with passion, perseverance and perspective can make the most of the change by creating new businesses and new business models that provide leadership to everyone else. By being unique and finding a niche, leaders who create these new paradigms of business will stand out and attract an audience.

However, no good idea comes to life on it's own. Great ideas are a dime-a-dozen, and having an idea without the passion to work at it and the perseverance to *keep* working at it is practically useless. The idea needs to be planned out and taken into action in order to come to life. That is the function of a business plan.

As mentioned earlier, a business plan basically maps out your vision for your business on paper with enough details to attract a potential investor. It clarifies how to start the business. It examines what the challenges and opportunities are within that business. But more importantly, it can guide you through all the details of running this business successfully *before* even trying!

Simply put, the business plan is the map to your career—the one you want to build for yourself. If the perfect job isn't knocking on your door (my guess is that it isn't—if it were, would you be reading this book?) then damn it, you'll just have to go build your own!

As passionate musical people, ideas are never that far away. Passion isn't either—we're very passionate about our love for music and audio, which is why we choose it for a career (or maybe it chooses us!). However, perseverance, forethought and planning can be in short supply for many of us. Worse, having the discipline to plan our actions and actually stick to the plan is even scarcer.

That's why the business plan is so necessary. Without it, we'd be frolicking around trying to launch our idea with no clue as to what dangers lurk around the corner. We'd attack the market with perhaps all the wrong tools, only to find that we've wasted our time, energy and worse—our precious money. Money is hard to come by so when it comes, you've got to make the most of it!

Paul Terry has been building business plans and consulting on businesses for over 20 years and his approach to sustainable business and its effect on communities is a welcome and refreshing approach in jaded times. In these next pages, Paul offers his insights into business planning as a general tool for use in any industry. He outlines the six sections of a good plan, what should go into those sections and more importantly—a checklist to see if you've got "what it takes" to build your own career.

Keep in mind that this is an introduction to business planning. In future volumes we will cover, in detail, how to build a business plan for your idea—starting with some simple ideas and building from there. What's important now is to understand each of the six sections of a plan and start formulating answers to them in your vision. And remember—just because your idea sounds good to you, that doesn't make it good. Do the work. Do the research. Ask (and answer) the tough questions.

And above all else, persevere.

—Matt Donner

17

The Business Plan—A Roadmap To Success

There are many people starting small businesses and almost as many failing. However, there is a way to reduce your risks and increase your chances of success for your own small business. The secret involves planning, research, developing, writing and using a business plan. Regardless of the sector of the music and audio industry you choose to pursue, a business plan is should be seen as a statistical and emotion-less fact-finding mission that acts as a litmus test for profitability. At the end of the day, if a business is not profitable it will not be able to sustain itself. Dreams and grandiose visions are a great starting place but are no substitute for a well-developed business plan.

Risk always exists in a small business! The ability to learn from mistakes and be open to new ideas is critical. However, risk can be reduced and opportunities can be measured, if time is set aside to define the business, do careful market research, develop key management skills, and create realistic financial expectations. Above all, you must recognize that a key factor for long-term business success is the *implementation* of the business plan. Completing, maintaining and implementing a business plan and then learning from your mistakes, is hard work.

"Genius is 1% inspiration and 99% perspiration."—Thomas Edison, inventor

"In the beginner's mind there are many possibilities; in the expert's mind, there are few."—Suzuki Roshi, Zen Buddhist teacher

Planning is learning to read the pulse of the business. However, small business owners are impatient. They want to get on with running the business and do not have or make time to write the business plan. Often they are intimidated or they simply procrastinate. It is true that some successful small businesses can start without any thought to planning and manage by reaction. However, once the business starts to get complicated, finding solutions can become confusing and a business plan can really help sort out the options, opportunities and problems—ahead of time.

What Is a Business Plan?

DVD: Studio-Side Chat
Business Plan versus
Marketing Plan: 14:44–16:32

Simply, a business plan is a written, objective analysis of the business *before* you actually build it. It is a roadmap, a blueprint for how to start it. It is your best attempt at predicting your future reality—a good plan will prepare the owner to take advantage of opportunities as they occur and to deal with problems by anticipating them in advance.

The primary purpose of a business plan is in the process itself. Writing a business plan forces you to be objective and critical about your vision. It helps you identify weaknesses and opportunities, suggests benchmarks to mark any progress and gives you confidence that you should (or should not!) continue to build this business.

There are other important reasons. The plan becomes an operational management tool that can be used to manage your ongoing business. It is also a means of communication to others about your business—partners, supporters, customers and friends. Finally, if appropriate, it can be used to raise capital for the business.

The business owner, owners or key management should write this plan. Only you have the unique perspective needed to understand the business you're trying to create and whether, in the end, it's going to be worth it. Of course you may need help or assistance from a professional, but the responsibility of creating the plan must remain with the business owner. If not, it becomes only a written exercise, not a useful document appropriate for planning.

A business plan should be a dynamic document—it needs to be current, accessible, and appropriate for the business. The planning process is both rational and intuitive. The written plan is a foundation from which each owner's business judgment, personal feelings, and intuition are measured. Since the business you create is also dynamic, the plan should be updated every so often to reflect changes in your business, changes in the market, new opportunities as well as new challenges. You should write it in such a way that you and others can see it, read it, and use it—daily, monthly, quarterly and review at least annually!

Keep in mind that a business plan does *not* guarantee success. It can help prevent serious mistakes, but it does not remove risk or predict the unknown. The business plan may be written well enough to raise money for your business but this same plan may not be written well enough to run your business successfully. The business plan is a document used to manage present and future opportunities and problems. The business plan is your plan to succeed!

Each business is different and, therefore, each business plan is going to be unique. However, a business planning process will create benchmarks and criteria that will be essential in evaluating the progress and success of your business. In the end, you will have a complete document that can be used to help you run your business, plan for the future and communicate to others: potential partners, investors and customers.

Am I An Entrepreneur? Key Questions & Personal Assessments

There are the key issues that every new small business owner must address if they're considering starting a business for the first time. Check the list below and see how you do with many of these questions. Look carefully at how you would review and solve many of the key challenges. [Put a number—1, 2, or 3 to gauge how strongly you feel about each point (3 being the strongest, 1 being the weakest). Total each section and compare it to the average—are you an entrepreneur?] Not all the above conditions need to be in place before you start exploring self-employment. However, these are issues that will be key for long-term success.

(Answer the questions and see what they tell you about yourself.)

1. Do I have what it takes to start my own small business?

You will be your own most important and first employee, so an objective analysis of your strengths and weaknesses is essential. You will need to make a realistic assessment of yourself.

Are you someone who:

☛ can launch something on your own?

☛ is a self starter and takes the initiative on new activities?

☛ can make good decisions when many options appear?

☛ has the necessary physical and emotional stamina to be self-employed and "on your own"?

☛ can plan and organize new data and existing information well?

☛ has a positive attitude about the future and a passion about a new business idea or being in business?

☛ has good support from your family and friends?

2. Do I have a business or business idea I want to develop?

Do you know what business you would want to start? Can you realistically assess whether an idea is viable for you and the marketplace? Do you know how to determine which idea may be the "best" for you?

The best business for you is one that requires that you have:

☛ a sincere interest and strong passion for what you will be doing.

☛ some of the skills that are needed to provide the service or build the product.

☛   a sustaining interest in doing a business like yours.

☛   some previous and related work experience.

☛   completed or are researching the potential of your kind of business.

☛   worked for someone who is doing something similar to what you would like to provide.

☛   some understanding of what the customer or client expects from your kind of business.

☛   confidence that your product or service is "needed" in the marketplace and can attract clients.

3.   Are you willing to deal with legal considerations?

You may be clear on your own motivation and preparedness, and you may have a business idea that makes sense to you, has a ready market, and is matched to your own personal skills. Now, what are the "legal" or "operational" issues that a new business owner must face?

Are you someone who will take the time to:

☛   research tax obligations and acquire licenses?

☛   satisfy any certification or training issues required *before* you open for business?

☛   set up an internal organizational system to track and monitor "legal" requirements?

☛   set up a professional team to help make business, legal and accounting decisions?

☛   design and use a bookkeeping system to give you reports and keep you current with regard to taxes?

Now that you've assessed your skills and risk tolerance level, you should consider the elements that makes some businesses successful and other businesses fail. There are some common factors among those who succeed as well as those who fail. Consider the following list:

The Basic Skills for Long-Term Success (aka Twenty Considerations for Long-Term Success)

1. Know yourself well. Don't pretend to be someone you are not.
2. Be very clear about your existing business skills.
3. Identify where you need more training or help from others.
4. Research and develop excellent small business resources—both general and industry-specific.
5. Nurture and expand personal and business networks to address isolation and lack of good information.
6. Understand what your business will actually do and be able to describe it to anyone at any time.
7. Be aware of the larger macro issues that may affect your small business—economics, technology, etc.
8. Obtain and expand the technical expertise/skills necessary to do the business or provide the service.
9. Acquire actual small business management experience— making and implementing decisions.
10. Understand simple market research techniques.
11. Do some market research every day to find and understand your targeted customer or client.
12. Spend time everyday looking for and understanding your competition.
13. Develop your ability to plan ahead and complete tasks on a timely, practical basis.
14. Set both simple and realistic goals for your new business that can be measured and are achieveable.
15. Have a good understanding of your own personal money matters.
16. Estimate how much actual cash you may need to launch your business.

17. Identify your money sources and raise the appropriate amount of seed capital that you require.
18. Make sure you are going to "love" making this product and/or delivering this service.
19. Schedule classes, workshops and trainings that help you continue your business education.
20. Keep records of everything you do, the money you spend and the taxes you may owe.

Use the checklist as a guide and follow both your heart and your head in launching a small business for the first time. It's hard work but very rewarding with each successful step!

The Six Basic Elements of a Business Plan

Each business plan is going to stress different areas of the business. However, every business plan has some or all of the elements discussed below.

Summary Review/Introduction

This will be the first section read and should give a synopsis of the most important factors of the business: the management skills, marketing focus and the use and projection of financial issues.

The introduction can be a brief narrative that introduces the business plan but really focuses on you, your philosophies, visions, goals and objectives on being in business. Here, you may also clarify the purpose of the business plan—a planning process, a management review and/or a request for investment.

The Business/Business History & Description of Products and Services

For an on-going business, you will include: management, ownership and capitalization history; legal form of business and the financial health of the business. For a new business, you should also include detail information about your specific industry: the current status, trends and potential opportunities. For any stage of business, it is also vital to know the importance of the broader aspects that include: cultural issues; environmental restrictions, technological impact and economic conditions.

A specific description of your business should be stated. You may have a product or provide a service that you manufacture, re-package or uniquely "display." Any details on how something works, is used or is applied should be clearly described. You should also mention any additional products or services that you propose to add as the business grows and becomes established.

The Marketing Plan

Before you can tell if there is a market (whether there are actually customers for your product or service), you must do research and analyze the results. You will want to convince first yourself and then any potential supporter that your products or services are of high quality, that there is an accepting and growing marketplace, that you will be able to achieve projected financial forecasts for your business and, even though there is competition, succeed.

Competition will always exist, both directly (a business with the same product/service) and indirectly (a business serving your targeted customers with similar services or products). It's important to recognize both direct and indirect competition, as well as to locate and measure that competition. If appropriate, you need to visit them and view their products and services to make realistic comparisons so you can identify your competitive advantages (and disadvantages!).

Not everyone in your geographic area is your targeted prime customer or client. The potential marketplace is too large for a small, emerging business. Industry analysis and competitive research will help you focus on a precise market that needs your products/services, will pay the price, finds the location convenient, responds to the promotion used and is willing to be loyal and repetitive over time. Targeting and serving a small market well is effective marketing.

Make sure you have researched the industry, checked out much of the competition, talked to vendors and knowledgeable people in the field and analyzed industry statistics. Then you can focus on your own target market and identify competitive advantages..

You'll want to have and use marketing strategies that will be unique and specific to your business, its "products" and the customer base that you have identified. This may include word-of-mouth, publicity, personal selling or advertising. Your tactics and strategies will also depend on price levels, a convenient location, trained personnel and any "packaging" or image requirements for your target market.

The Management Plan

Your ownership and management team is the key to success. There must be adequate skills to match the complexity of the business. Owner, manager and key personnel must be clearly identified. All support personnel and business advisors are also important!

If your products or services need to be "produced" or "packaged" in any way, there will be considerable operational factors such as supply sources, lead times and production lines to consider. Each of these matters will need to be researched with vendors identified and timelines managed. Both services and products need to have operational procedures. For a service business, this may include contract negotiation, interviews, bids, provision of service, completion of the "product", delivery and final payment, as well as referrals to more work and a long-term relationship.

The Financial Plan

A key aspect of of your business plan is the financial plan. Your financial information must translate your management and marketing assumptions. For an existing business, historical financial information must be analyzed. The subsequent projections will create benchmarks for the owner to measure progress and will be used to inform potential investors. For a new or emerging business, information can be gleaned from industry data, competitive research or experience from prior work experience.

The financial data should clearly state how much money will be made, how much will be needed to run the business and when it will be needed. Financial projections must be realistic and not deviate from past experience or industry standards unless they can be clearly justified. Pro forma statements need to include a balance sheet, income statement, cash flow statement, and a source and use funds statement. The information and assumptions used to develop pro forma statements need to be clear, well documented, and realistic if the business plan is to be viable.

The Development Plan

The business owner must take the initiative to identify and discuss inherent risks of the business. This will increase the potential investors confidence (and minimize loss of credibility when the investor discovers a negative factor that has been overlooked). Look at potential risks for your business, discuss them openly and make plans that will minimize their impact on your business.

It is also important to understand growth for your business. Describe an appropriate scenario for growth and plan the timing, implementation and impact. You must plan for growth so it doesn't overcome your business. Growth planning will help you plan for the reality before it becomes overwhelming and/or catches you unprepared.

Once the business plan is complete, how will it get implemented? The business owner needs to follow the timelines, objectives and goals so that the business will really get started or expand. Every business needs a specific and unique plan of action to bring the business to fruition. The owner must commit to do it!

18

The Business Plan, Detailed

The Basic One-Page Outline

DVD: Studio-Side Chat
Business Plan versus
Marketing Plan: 14:44–16:32

Every business plan should start with an outline, explaining to the reader what to expect. As you might imagine, it should be sectioned off according to the six basic sections of a business plan. **Figure 17** is a generic example of a business plan's one-page outline.

Sample Business Plan Outline

I.   Introduction
      A. Executive Summary
      B. Introduction to Your Business Plan

II.   The Business
      A. History of the Current Business (if an existing business)—or—
      B. Overview of the Proposed Business
      C. Introduction to Products/Services

III. The Marketing Plan
      A. The Marketplace
      B. The Competition
      C. Targeting Your Market
      D. Marketing Strategies
      E. Implementation

IV.   The Management Plan
      A. Manufacturing & Operations
      B. Ownership/Personnel
      C. Legalities and Certifications
      D. Technology Plan

V.   The Financial Plan
      A. Introduction
      B. Overview & Purpose
      C. Financial Narrative
      D. Financial Statements
      E. Funding Needs & Options

VI.   Analysis & Business Development
      A. Business Risk Analysis
      B. Growth/Expansion
      C. Implementation & Action Plan

VII. Appendix

Figure 17: *A generic example of an outline used for a business plan.*

The Introduction

Page two of your plan should begin digging into the details. The outline should be followed by the introduction. Think of it like this—if someone needs to read the *whole* business plan in order to understand your business, you really don't understand it yourself. The introduction basically goes back to the "elevator pitch" concept—you've got 30 seconds to pitch your idea to a potential investor while you ride up in an elevator together.

The introduction is basically a written elevator pitch—you've got one or two pages to pique the interest of your reader. If they don't get the idea on these two pages and are not interested at this time, they're out. To be sure you're nailing it, the introduction should be written last—after you've fleshed out ALL the other points and have a very clear vision of the plan. This way, you can boil the plan down to its essence and deliver a crisp and concise introduction. Make it engaging, snappy and exciting, but get to the point—quickly.

Executive Summary

Some of the key points that the Executive Summary should cover include the following: (Mind you, not all will apply to your business so keep it short and sweet. Try not to write it bullet-by-bullet, but rather fit as much data as you can in a narrative form that is exciting to the reader.)

☛ Mission or Purpose: What are your goals? Why are you starting this business?

☛ Products and Services: What do you sell? What services will you offer?

☛ Target Market(s): Prioritize the markets you serve or intend to reach, and why.

☛ Marketing and Sales Strategy: How will you reach your target market(s)? Advertising? Direct mail? Trade shows? Word of mouth?

☛ Management & Expertise: Who's on your team? Why do they deserve it?

☛ Operations/Manufacturing: How does your business work? How do you make/service your product/client?

☞ Financials: Now that they know how much, show them (briefly) why that's the right number.

☞ Implementation or action plan: The plan is step one. What's step two? Three? Eighteen?

Introduction to the Business Plan

This narrative section focuses on you and your reasons or purpose for being in business—why do you want to do this? It provides an opportunity for you to clarify the value of your business plan as a planning process, as an opportunity to review management, and/or as a proposal for potential for investment. Even though the title is "Introduction to the Business Plan," the real purpose of this section is you. Most investors don't invest in ideas—they invest in people. Here's where you sell them on why you're the right person for this idea and this plan.

Some of the questions you'll need to answer here include:

☞ What is your vision or purpose in starting and expanding this business?

☞ What fuels your desire to be self-employed and why right now?

☞ Do you have a goal for where you want to be one year from today?

☞ Do you have specific and related prior experience (direct work, experience, study or hobby) that has prepared you to start or expand this business?

☞ What are your current strengths as a new or would-be business owner? Weaknesses?

The Business

. . . .

History of the Current Business

Since this book is meant as an introduction to business concepts, we'll assume that you don't have an existing business with a history that would need to be included in your plan.

Overview of Proposed Business

This is the section where you explain the industry you're in (music and audio) and what function your business will serve in this industry. If your business is a start-up, include the details about your specific industry. Mainly, this section is your take on the "State of the Union" and how your business will be formed within this union. Make sure to include the following:

☛ What are the current conditions of this industry (including economic, social, technological, etc.) and what impact will the current status of your industry have on your individual business?

☛ What legal form of business (i.e., sole proprietorship, partnership, corporation, etc.) will you choose? Why would you choose this form of business structure?

☛ Describe your proposed business. (A 25-word summary should be enough)

Introduction to Products/Services

Every new or existing business offers a product or service and some offer both. Whether you have a product you manufacture, distribute or display in a retail or e-business environment, or a service you provide to the industry, it needs to be clearly described in this section of your plan. Be specific about which sector in the music and audio industry you'll be entering, (production, distribution, artistic development, licensing, etc.) Mention any additional products or services that you propose to add as the business grows. If you have a service business, note any key factors that distinguish your service from your competition.

Describe in detail your product line or range of services and how they compare to the competition—your advantages and disadvantages. Provide details on the range or variety of products and/or services offered. What opportunities do you propose to initiate, change or improve as your business grows? How will the business be ready for new opportunities regarding management, marketing or financial readiness?

The Marketing Plan

The Marketplace: Who are Your Customers? Are There Any?

As mentioned previously, to determine if there's a market for your product or service, you must research opportunities and analyze the competition. You need to convince yourself and any supporter that your products are of high quality, that there is an accepting and growing marketplace for them, that you will be able to achieve your projected forecasts for your business, and that even with competition, you will succeed. This may be one of the hardest sections to work on because it will force you to understand who your clients and customers are.

In the music and audio industry, there are many sectors to explore and plenty of clients out there but the important question you need to answer is—are there enough of them to make you profitable?. . . get their attention. (You might want to spend more time on this section than others.) Many a great idea has failed due to a lack of qualified customers or worse—an inability to understand their needs and how to get their attention. You might spend more time here than in the other sections.

Try to answer some hard questions. What constitutes your total potential marketplace or customer base? Give an overview of this market including market trends. Can you determine what your total market is, i.e., where all your potential customers and competition exist? How is your total market affected by macro issues such as economics, environmental issues, business cycles and/or technological change? Be clear how these larger issues could affect your emerging business.

The Competition

As stated earlier, competition will always exist, either direct (someone else sells just what you sell at another location) or indirect (other people serving the same pool of customers with similar services). It is important to identify who your direct competitors are, where they are located, what their competitive factors are, and if there is any direct competition. After all, opening another one of those businesses is no guarantee of success. If there are five games in town, what's going to make the marketplace move away from them to you? Will you have better gear? Cheaper rates? Better service? How can you prove it?

☛ Describe the maturity, size, location and success of your direct and indirect competition or one typical direct competitor. (What are the competition's weaknesses, strengths, and opportunities?)

☛ Describe what you think may be your distinct advantages and disadvantages. (How would you compete against such direct competitors listed above?)

☛ Identify how—or if—you can use the competition as a resource. (Can you approach competitors as a source of information, for joint ventures, or to get referrals?)

Targeting Your Market

Once you've researched the industry, checked out much of the competition, talked to vendors and knowledgeable people in the field, analyzed industry statistics, and identified a potential target market, how exactly are you going to find your customers? Better yet—how will they find *you*? Define your target markets, customers, their locations and their buying habits.

Marketing Strategies

You know they're there, you know there's room for your business and you know where your customers are. Now you need to explain just how you'll get their attention.

☛ Describe the products or services you will offer and their pricing structures.

☛ Define issues of place—either location or distribution.

☛ Explain your commitment to customer service.

☛ Describe your promotional plans for word-of-mouth publicity and advertising.

☛ Talk about personal selling and sales personnel including strategies and tactics.

☛ Describe how you will measure and monitor your marketing strategies—the metrics!

Market Implementation

The marketing plan requires an implementation strategy. Consider what goals you are trying to achieve and what strategies will help you reach that goal. Set up action steps that can be achieved within a realistic timeline and affordable budget.

☛ What are your initial marketing goals? (They must be S.M.A.R.T.— Specific, Measurable, Attainable, Realistic, and Timely.)

☛ What are the best strategies and actions necessary to reach these goals? How long will this take?

☛ What additional resources may be needed and how much will they cost?

The Management Plan

Operations

Several systems are needed to manage your general business operations, including bookings, client management and information, billing, collections, and hiring contractors, among others. In this section, list the operations that your business will have to engage in and how you plan to manage all of these functions. Try to be detailed—choose specific tools, versions and workflows.

You'll likely need to invest in some startup equipment (computers, desks, software licenses etc.) so discuss them here but save the money details for the financing sections. In addition, list any upgrades you have to make to the physical space that you've chosen to operate from If you have no space yet, describe the needs of the space and what it might cost to outfit that space to your business.

Ownership/Personnel

Good managers are the key to success! As an owner and manager of your own business, you must use previous business experience, build the expertise from practice, and develop a wide range of skills. You'll need to detail your current management expertise and past management experience as well as a list of your teammates, advisors and peer support. You'll also need to describe your organizational and personnel structure including:

☛ Job descriptions with compensation and benefits

☛ Your philosophy regarding authority, decision making, and power sharing.

☛ An organization chart if available and helpful to the understanding of business process.

Legalities and Certifications

For every new and existing business, there are legal considerations. Note here what you know you need and how you have covered such legalities.

☛ Local licensing and fictitious business name filing.

☛ Additional certification or licensing if required by your industry.

☛ If you have or are consulting a legal advisor.

☛ Any insurance coverage you have or insurance advice you've received.

☛ Any contracts you may need to protect your legal rights.

☛ Intellectual property issues such as trademarks, service mark, copyrights or patents or trade secrets.

Technology Plan

To keep your business fully functioning, you must have a technology plan to cover customer information and follow-ups, breakdowns and expansions and regular maintenance on both the systems and information. Explain your technology plan here.

The Financial Plan

Introduction

As mentioned earlier, the financial section of the business plan is where "the rubber meets the road." All the assumptions about the business, its products and services, the past and potential success in the marketplace are quantified here. In the following sections be prepared to justify EVERY cost and EVERY revenue assumption—pretty numbers in charts are great, but they're useless if they are unrealistic.

The financial data should clearly state how much money will be made, how much will be needed for the business and when. Financial projections must be realistic. The projections must also include any assumptions made within the business plan including marketing projections, personnel commissions, new locations, or expansion of production. Quotes from experts in the field, friendly competitors, and professionals will be helpful in verifying assumptions.

Financial Narrative

Your business plan assumes your business will grow at a certain rate, attract specific numbers of customers, sell a specific volume of product, bill extensive hours, and employ a variety of strategies (marketing, management, and operations) with associated costs to achieve your goals. *You MUST include a financial narrative that describes all of this.* This narrative will sit in the body of the text, and summarize information from the detailed financials.

Your financial narrative will summarize the past history (if you have an existing business) and current status of the business, your own personal investment, and other potential investments that may be needed. Use your financial narrative summary to quantify the assumptions made regarding sales, overhead expenses, capital needs, and any draw that you intend to take from your business.

Your financial narrative summary should clearly state how much money you will need to start and continue to operate your business in contrast to the amount of money you expect your business to make on a regular basis. You will need to refer to your spreadsheets that contain estimates of your start-up costs and income/expense projections. In addition, your financial narrative should state how any money invested in the business is going to be used and how it will be repaid.

Details on Financial Statements

Start-Up Costs Report: This statement is simply a list of all costs that need to be incurred before the business is opened. For an existing business, you would prepare an "expansion" report. This list includes tangible assets such as equipment, furniture, leasehold improvements and inventory; or intangible assets such as critical marketing collateral. There may also be start-up costs ONLY related to new businesses, such as licenses, insurance, bonding, permits, office supplies, and professional assistance.

Figure 18 provides a chart of potential start-up costs.

Start Up Costs

COSTS	ESTIMATE	RESOURCE FOR INFORMATION
General		
License/Permit	$100.00	City & County offices
Start-up Marketing	$500.00	Printer or Graphic artist
Bookkeeping/Accounting	$750.00	Accountant, books, or software
Legal Advice/Contracts	$500.00	Legal referral service
Prepaid Insurance	$750.00	Insurance agent
Capital Reserve	$2,000.00	Banker or own Review
Other		
Subtotal for General	$4,600.00	
Location Issues		
Rent or Security Deposit	$1,500.00	Landlord/self
Remodeling/Leasehold	$3,000.00	Contractor/Materials cost
Telephone installation	$250.00	Telephone Company
Computer	$1,500.00	Retailers/Want ads
Furniture/Equipment	$500.00	Retailers/Used dealers
Office Supplies	$150.00	Office Supply Store
Other		
Other		
Subtotal for Location	$6,900.00	
Product Businesses		
Manufacturing (materials for 3 months)	$5,000.00	Wholesalers or vendors
Retail (start-up inventory)	$5,000.00	Wholesalers, vendors, or estimate
Tools/equipment	$1,000.00	Borrow, make, or buy
Personnel	$1,000.00	Temp agency or part-time staff
Subtotal for Products	$12,000.00	
Other Costs		
TOTAL START UP COSTS	$23,500.00	

Figure 18: *Potential startup costs.*

The Pro Forma Statement: In this case, *pro forma* means "as a matter of form" or "average." As it's likely that your business hasn't started yet, you can't show any actual numbers based on history, so you'll have to present numbers based on an average use level. You will have to make assumptions about costs, revenue and customer satisfaction and then use those "average" numbers to generate a financial document.

Projected Profit and Loss Statement: This financial statement reflects all of the assumptions that you have gathered from marketing research, competitor analysis, sales estimates, and cost comparisons. Here is where your sales "guesstimates", (your marketing strategic action plan and your associated cost estimates) meet and debate for reality. You will have collected information on all relevant costs of goods and overhead expenses for the business. You should also know how much money you (and/or your partner) will need to "draw" from the business.

If you are not yet in business, it is acceptable to prepare your 24-month profit and loss projection as shown in **Figure 19**. For those of you who are already in business, you may include some historical information in the first twelve months of the profit and loss statement. However, the second twelve months would be a projection.

Whether you are already in business or not, refer to your completed market research as you prepare the sales estimate portions of the profit and loss projection. Prepare appropriate footnotes explaining all relative items contained in your 24-month projections.

Sources and Uses of Funds: It's important to include both a detailed narrative and financial statement indicating how you plan to raise any of the money you need (including money you plan to contribute, loans, or equity) as well as how the funds will be used (equipment, leasehold improvements, inventory, or working capital). This statement will confirm where you plan to get money, how likely it is that you will actually get it, and prioritize when and how you plan to use it.

Detailed Footnotes on Assumptions (financial narrative): However clear an idea may seem to you, make sure you back it up with your reasoning and any useful data. Each critical assumption in all financial statements must have a written footnote to explain your assumptions. As you work through

Simple Business Projections
Product Business

Description	Month 1	Month 2	Month 3	Month 4	Month 5	Month 6	Month 7	Month 8	Month 9	Month 10	Month 11	Month 12	TOTAL	%%%
REVENUE														
Rentals	4,500	5,000	5,500	6,000	5,500	6,000	6,500	5,000	5,500	6,500	7,000	7,500	**70,500**	57.7%
Services	2,500	3,000	3,000	3,000	3,500	3,500	3,500	4,000	4,000	3,500	3,500	4,000	**41,000**	33.6%
Products	500	800	1,000	1,000	1,000	700	800	900	1,000	1,000	1,000	1,000	**10,700**	8.8%
TOTAL SALES	7,500	8,800	9,500	10,000	10,000	10,200	10,800	9,900	10,500	11,000	11,500	12,500	122,200	100.0%
COSTS OF GOODS														
Rentals	900	1,000	1,100	1,200	1,100	1,200	1,300	1,000	1,100	1,300	1,400	1,500	**14,100**	11.5%
Labor/Personnel	875	1,050	1,050	1,050	1,225	1,225	1,225	1,400	1,400	1,225	1,225	1,400	**14,350**	11.7%
Product Costs	125	200	250	250	250	175	200	225	250	250	250	250	**2,675**	2.2%
TOTAL COGS	1,900	2,250	2,400	2,500	2,575	2,600	2,725	2,625	2,750	2,775	2,875	3,150	31,125	25.5%
GROSS PROFIT	5,600	6,550	7,100	7,500	7,425	7,600	8,075	7,275	7,750	8,225	8,625	9,350	91,075	74.5%
OP EXPENSES														
Accounting	125	125	125	425	125	425	125	125	425	125	125	425	**2,700**	2.2%
Insurance	200	200	200	200	200	200	200	200	200	200	200	200	**2,400**	2.0%
Marketing	250	350	450	250	350	450	350	450	550	450	550	650	**5,100**	4.2%
Misc	50	50	50	50	50	50	50	50	50	50	50	50	**600**	0.5%
Personnel	1,500	1,500	1,500	2,000	2,000	2,000	2,500	2,500	2,500	3,000	3,500	4,000	**28,500**	23.3%
Rent	2,500	2,500	2,500	2,500	2,500	2,500	2,500	2,500	2,500	2,500	2,500	2,500	**30,000**	24.5%
Supplies	150	150	150	150	150	150	150	150	150	150	150	150	**1,800**	1.5%
Telephone	200	200	200	250	250	250	300	300	300	400	400	400	**3,450**	2.8%
Travel	75	75	75	75	75	75	75	75	75	75	75	75	**900**	0.7%
TOTAL OP EXPENSES	5,050	5,150	5,250	5,900	5,700	6,100	6,250	6,350	6,750	6,950	7,550	8,450	75,450	61.7%
OPERATING PROFIT	550	1,400	1,850	1,600	1,725	1,500	1,825	925	1,000	1,275	1,075	900	15,625	12.8%

Sample Profit and Loss

Figure 19: *A Basic P&L Structure.*

each financial statement, keep track (on paper or in word processing) of what you did to get the numbers. Your final pro forma statements should include footnotes of all your assumptions.

Example: Include the information listed below as a financial narrative in the body of the text and footnotes within the statement:

"Based on competitive research and some actual experience, I can bill $60/hour and bill at least 2 hours per day, 5 days per week, and 10 months per year. For each month I am in business, I estimate adding one more client to a maximum of 10 per month."

Samples of key expense items only such as:

☞ Marketing costs including Website design, mailing costs and one brochure. Costs included only in the months that they occur.

☞ Administrative costs including office expenses and hiring part-time labor (for shipping needs) in October, November and December only.

☞ Rent is $500 per month based on an average rate of $2.00/ square foot for 250 square feet. (Rent increases of 10% per year are also assumed.)

Funding Needs & Options

If you are going to raise funds from others, you want to include a narrative that points out why they would choose to give you their money, otherwise known as "investment opportunities." In this case, please list any anticipated return on investment, loan interest rates, investment amounts needed, limited partnership alternatives, and/or corporate shares available (if appropriate).

If you can *not* raise the money you need, indicate in a narrative how you could cut costs and still be able to start and/ or expand. (This may be indicated in your estimated start-up statement.)

Analysis & Business Development

Risk Analysis

All small businesses are at risk most of the time. Therefore, the business owner must take the initiative to identify and discuss inherent risks to increase any potential investor confidence. Below are examples of common risks. Pick those that are appropriate to you and your business. If those listed below are not appropriate to you, add other categories that explain the risk to your business. Then, discuss your strategies to minimize those risks.

Lack of management experience
Description:

Mitigation strategies:

The effect of competition—direct and/or indirect
Description:

Mitigation strategies:

Seasonality of the work or fluctuation of revenue payments due to client's cash flow policies
Description:

Mitigation strategies:

Time management, and/or personal motivation, isolation and burnout
Description:

Mitigation strategies:

Undercapitalization and/or lack of initial cash for start-up
Description:

Mitigation strategies:

The need to grow slowly and not expand too quickly, and its impact on sales or profitability
Description:

Mitigation strategies:

Financial records preparation and understanding of month-end statements
Description:

Mitigation strategies:

Sourcing, distance, timing, and/or other distribution factors
Description:

Mitigation strategies:

Any other risks for you and your business
Description:

Mitigation strategies:

Growth/Expansion

From start-up to maturity, each business must confront the issues of growth and stagnation even if that means flat sales for one accounting period. Growing a business and preparing for growth are important strategic issues to understand. Here are some important questions to ask as you address growth for your business:

☛ How do you define growth for your business?

Growth can be defined by size, increased sales, higher profits, more clients, and/or more employees.

☛ Why do you want to grow your business?

Businesses grow for a variety of reasons including competition, an exciting vision, or a new opportunity.

☛ What can you do to prepare to grow?

Preparation for growth begins at start-up and includes planning, conducting research, getting more education, finding a partner.

☛ Which methodology will help you grow?

Growth strategies include product diversification, specialized targeting, or client expansion.

☛ What are important benchmarks for growth?

Planning should be S.M.A.R.T.: Specific, Measurable, Attainable, Realistic, and Timely.)

☛ What specific benchmarks for growth have you defined?

(See first bullet point above)

Implementation & Action Plan

Every business should have a specific and unique plan of action. Once the business plan is complete, how will you implement it? Use a specific and visual technique (e.g., Excel spreadsheet) to quantify goals and give timelines that indicate completion date so that the business will really get started and/or expand.

☛ What timelines and/or milestone charts will you use to plan and project business actions? (See **Figure 20** for example.)

Monthly Milestone Chart

Month	1	2	3	4	5	6	7	8	9	10	11	12
Objectives /Tasks												
Marketing Related												
1.												
2.												
3.												
4.												
5.												
Management Related												
Finance Related												
1.												
2.												
3.												
4.												
5.												
Other												
1.												
2.												
3.												
4.												
5.												

Figure 20: *shows a Milestone chart across the various sectors of a business plan.*

☛ How will you implement the business plan and what schedule do you estimate on a step-by-step basis? (Explain how to break down each step, in order, and follow a clear set of priorities.)

☛ Note all critical dates for implementation of your business. (For example, business needs to be open by the fall; have equipment operational by a specific date; samples ready for distribution in two weeks; capital approved by July 15th, etc.)

☛ What alternative plans/actions are in place in case of delays? (Are there ways to start with less capital; can you start with small accounts or limited hours?)

☛ How will you set benchmarks and metrics and then monitor your progress? (What benchmarks have you set by date, sales level, profitability, etc., to measure financial success or market stability?)

CHAPTER 19

The Business Plan FAQ

Ten Essential Questions

1. **What qualities do I need to have to successfully start my own small business?**

As a new small business owner, you will be your first and most important employee. So, it is key that you complete an objective and honest inventory of your strengths and weaknesses. It will be important to know if you are someone who can launch something on your own; able to make decisions well; has both physical and emotional stamina; can plan and organize your time well; has a positive attitude; and perhaps most importantly, has a real passion for the business that you want to start; can stay motivated; and has great support and backing from your family and friends.

2. **What business skills would be helpful to have before starting?**

You must be clear about your real motivation for being in business as this will help in all stages of growth. You will need to assess your past business-related and inter-personal skills to see how well you are prepared before starting. You could also identify and compare personality and business traits common to successful entrepreneurs. These traits are personal attributes that are important for anyone to have who is starting or running a small business. This can include persistence and full commitment to doing what is needed; having the ability to face facts of the marketplace; being able to minimize risks as you start and grow; being well organized for all operations; being a hands-on learner as you take on new risks; and being able to understand and use the "numbers" of a business.

3. What business should I choose? How do I know I have a viable business idea?

The best business for anyone is going to be the one in which you are most skilled and interested, in which you have some previous experience and in which there is a need that you can fill well—if not better than anyone else. Most importantly, do what you love and the passion and interest will help the money to follow. You need to research the growth potential of various businesses. Matching your background with the local market will increase your chance of success. You can gain confidence and be realistic about your specific business idea if you can test it as something that is timely and appropriate (for the economy and your industry); is right for you (your personality and skills); matches your level of commitment (motivation and interest) and is clear and concise to others (easy to understand)

4. How do I define my business now and in the future if it continues to change?

The initial and never-ending question is, "What business am I really in?" New owners have failed because they never answered that question, or did not continue to ask it as the business changed. One owner realized that most of her income came from consulting while most of her time was tied up in writing articles. By "focusing" on the right source of income, she dramatically increased her profits. Defining and re-defining the business is a never-ending process from start-up through all stages of growth. It is critical to pay attention to your business as it changes and evolves. It will.

5. What is a business plan and why do I need one?

The business plan is an objectively written document that will help you plan your steps in advance. It asks, you "where am I going, how am I getting there and what do I need to prepare in advance?" A business plan precisely defines your business, identifies your goals and serves as your roadmap. It helps you allocate resources properly, handle unforeseen complications and make the right decisions before the crisis hits. The basic components include business description of products and/or services, a clear marketing direction and a plan to get there, defined management and operational concerns, a careful analysis of risk and pro forma financial statements reflecting where you are going in objective, realistic and practical terms.

6. What about outside help or mentors?

Building a team of peer supporters, industry experts, and senior mentors is an essential ingredient for any start-up business owner. Business owners want to talk with other start-up entrepreneurs—both within their industry and in other businesses. Talking to other business owners and even competitors is the best source of realistic business information and support. Other business owners and experts are often willing to be interviewed and offer advice—both informally as well as in formal advisory teams.

7. How much money do I need to get started?

Start-up capital will depend on the level and complexity of the business—from home-based music composing to complex manufacturing. You may also need money on hand to cover operating expenses for at least a year. These expenses include your draw as the owner and money to repay your loans. One commonly stated cause of business failure is inadequate start-up capital. It needs to match the needs of your business with your ability to reach your market. Estimating initial capital must include start-up costs, an estimate to cover any cash flow short-falls, and something in reserve.

8. What are the alternatives in raising capital?

Committing your own funds is often the first financing step. It is certainly the best indicator of how serious you are about your business. You are your first manager, employee, customer and your first investor; therefore you should see the value. Risking your own money gives confidence for others to invest in your business. You may want to consider a partner for additional financing or approach friends and supporters with a business-like promissory note and business plan. Banks are an obvious source of funds. Trade credit, selling stock, and equipment leasing offer alternatives to borrowing if you have industry experience as a new business owner.

9. Is starting with a partner a good idea?

For a start-up, a business partner is an excellent way to complement whatever skills you may consider yourself lacking. If you require additional management skills or start-up capital, engaging a partner may be your best decision. Personality and character, as well as ability to give technical or financial assistance, determine the ultimate success of a partnership. Of course, there must be a written agreement between you before you start.

10. What does marketing involve and how important is marketing to a start-up business?

Marketing is a very important aspect of your new business. There must be a need in the marketplace that you can serve. You must be as good as or better than the competition and you must find a target market or market niche where you can be competitive and serve the clients and customers well and often. There are six basic variables or strategies in planning your marketing and each must be understood and used appropriately to define and reach you customers and clients. They are called the marketing mix or the "six p's" of marketing:

The first is the **product**—the quality, consistency and uniqueness of product item or service you sell.

Next is **price**—the amount you charge for your product or service—considering your cost, competitive factors and what the "market" will pay for it.

Next is **promotion**—this is how you inform your market as to who you are, what you offer, where you're located, when you are available and how they can reach you.

Your location or **place** is the next part of the marketing mix—the location and distribution methods for your product or service. This could be retail, on-line, wholesale distribution, site visits or mail order—all depending on the type of business and the expectations of the client or customer.

It is important to include **packaging**—the way the business is "put together"—how the business appears to the public; the way it looks, from the promotional materials to the dress of the owner and the "style or culture" of the business.

Finally, it's **personnel**—the level of customer service you give and what sales or personality is communicated face-to-face or on the phone.

An Essential Plan for Success

Writing a business plan is not necessarily a guarantee of success, but *not* having one is almost always a guarantee of failure. Without the planning and foresight to plan out your business, the odds of you actually succeeding shrink dramatically. This is because you cannot accurately (or even closely) predict the financial requirements of your company ahead of time. This problem manifests in a few ways—

☛ You either fold before you open because you don't have enough money to open the business the way you thought. Setting out to build a $10 million studio without actually having $10 million or more is a good guarantee that you won't open the doors.

☛ You have enough to build the studio but not enough to actually run it. You spent all of your money building the studio with no staff, no management, no infrastructure, no marketing and not surprisingly—no customers.

☛ You built the studio, you launched the campaign and you hired staff but your campaign didn't work and now you're broke. Again, not surprisingly, you're ready for business with no customers.

☛ Okay—you've built the studio, hired the staff, launched the campaign and finally, the customers are coming in! Now, you realize that although they are coming in, they're not coming in fast enough to actually keep you in business. You're about to have the longest 6 months of your life trying to keep the place afloat as you now realize that you don't have enough operating capital to keep the place open.

Writing the plan is the job of the owner whether or not the plan is to be funded by yourself or someone else. It should be clearly written so your potential investor is not only excited by it, but believe in its promise and thus give you the money! It should also, like your résumé, be considered a living document. It will need constant tweaking and changing to reflect changes in the business environment, the market, technology, your staff and your desires.

No matter the business, your business plan is a MUST-HAVE. Spend the right time working on it and do your homework. Study the market and your would-be competition to see how they do business. This will either tell you what they're doing wrong *or* they'll tell you that there's just no room for you in the market. This can save you a lifetime of woes from trying to enter a business that just can't compete.

Rest assured, if you don't do your homework regarding your competition, they are surely doing their homework on you!

—*Paul Terry*

Index